This Is Spinal Tap

GW00391576

This Is Spinal Tap

John Kenneth Muir

AN IMPRINT OF HAL LEONARD CORPORATION

Copyright © 2010 by John Kenneth Muir

All rights reserved. No part of this book may be reproduced in any
form, without written permission, except by a newspaper or magazine
reviewer who wishes to quote brief passages in connection with a review.

Published in 2010 by Limelight Editions
An Imprint of Hal Leonard Corporation
7777 West Bluemound Road
Milwaukee, WI 53213

Trade Book Division Editorial Offices
33 Plymouth St., Montclair, NJ 07042

All photos courtesy of the author's collection

Printed in the United States of America

Book design by Mark Lerner

Library of Congress Cataloging-in-Publication Data is available upon
request.

ISBN 978-0-87910-377-4

www.limelighteditions.com

To Kathryn and Joel, who help me through
my own occasional *Spinal Tap* moments

CONTENTS

ACKNOWLEDGMENTS

As always, my gratitude begins with June Clark, an agent of uncommon valor and dedication, and a buddy to boot. My most humble thanks also go to the cast and crew of *This Is Spinal Tap*—but especially to Harry Shearer, June Chadwick, Fred Willard, director of photography Peter Smokler, actress Gloria Gifford, and film editor Kent Beyda, all of whom I spoke with in 2004 and 2005.

And lastly, my hat is off to Joe Franklin—the King of Nostalgia! Thanks for helping out, Joe.

This Is Spinal Tap

CHAPTER 1

Too Much F-ing Perspective
Remembering *This Is Spinal Tap* (1984)

The greatest rock 'n' roll band in the world is the Rolling Stones, at least according to *Gimme Shelter* (1970).

But Spinal Tap is still the loudest. . . .

A full quarter-century after its genesis, Rob Reiner's remarkable silver screen directorial debut, *This Is Spinal Tap,* remains an inescapable, nay *insurmountable* bump on the American pop culture highway.

This eighty-two-minute music-themed comedy from the mid-1980s yet shines, not only as an authentic Generation X touchstone but also as the undeniable gold standard of the cinematic format termed the "mockumentary," or what *Tap* coarchitect Christopher Guest often dubs a "documentary-style comedy."

What this description means is that *This Is Spinal Tap* poses as an authentic documentary, and is composed and edited in the cinema verité school down to the inclusion of archival footage in the B-roll (supplemental footage intercut with the main shots during interviews), "confessional" one-on-one interviews, and the sense that everything is unfolding before the camera "as live." But don't be fooled. Every moment in the film is purely fictional, made up from whole cloth: a mock (meaning "aped" or "simulated") reality.

Rock 'n' roll movies such as Mark Wahlberg's *Rock Star* (2002); parodies of the music industry including the Chris Rock vehicle *CB-4* (1993); mock rockumentaries like the Canadian *FUBAR* (2002); and real documentaries such as *Anvil! The Story of Anvil* (2009) attempt to recapture *Spinal Tap*'s revolutionary, inspired alchemy—at least after a fashion—but somehow, they never quite pull it off.

As movie critic Patrick Douglas noted in May 2005, the Reagan-era collaboration between comedian-actors Christopher Guest, Michael McKean, Rob Reiner, and Harry Shearer is likely to remain forever "the be-all and end-all of rock movies."[1] Consequently, *This Is Spinal Tap*'s accolades are nearly too numerous to catalog. But heck, let's give it a whirl.

In 1992, *Entertainment Weekly* ranked the Rob Reiner film as the third funniest in cinema history. It placed behind *Airplane!* (1980) and *Some Like It Hot* (1959) and nosed ahead of Woody Allen's Academy Award winner *Annie Hall* (1977). The magazine wrote: "First time director Rob Reiner's knowing mockumentary of a band of heavy-metal bozos gets everything right—even tiny details like the contents of a backstage deli tray. That the songs . . . are this clever and genuine bespeaks the creators' grasp of the essential ingredient for classic satire: a deep affection for the subject of ridicule."[2]

In 2002, the National Film Registry in the Library of Congress officially added *This Is Spinal Tap* to its rolls, honoring the production as one of the select few titles in a hundred years of movies—alongside such luminaries as *From Here to Eternity* (1953), *In the Heat of the Night* (1967), and *Alien* (1979)—to boast a critical trifecta: aesthetic, cultural, and historical significance.

At the time of *Spinal Tap*'s induction, Steve Leggett of the National Film Preservation Board told *Daily Variety*'s Paula McClintock that the film was selected because it had successfully "nailed a whole culture."[3] Beyond that, Leggett reported that *Spinal Tap* had also outgrown its own original context as a filmed entertainment of the "greed is good" Reagan decade, and that the term "spinal tap" had even come to have a larger social significance, particularly in the realm of politics. Legislation "that isn't what it seems to be is called '*spinal tap*,'"[4] he further explained.

In 2003, *Rolling Stone* magazine dubbed *This Is Spinal Tap* the "number one rock-and-roll movie of all time." Two years later, a *Blender* magazine poll saw the Reiner film win for a second time the honor of best rock movie in history, edging out the intimate *Metallica: Some Kind of Monster* (2004) and even Martin Scorsese's classic, loving ode to The Band, *The Last Waltz* (1978).

Similarly, in May 2005, *Mojo* magazine named *Tap* "the best music film of all time." It beat out the Beatles' seminal *A Hard Day's Night* (1964), the Stones' tragic and dark *Gimme Shelter*, and the expressionistic, psychedelic Alan Parker effort, *Pink Floyd The Wall* (1982).

In 2008, *Rolling Stone* held a poll for favorite "fake" or fictional band and Spinal Tap once more placed first, beating out Wild Stallyns (*Bill & Ted's Excellent Adventure* [1989]), the Commitments from the movie of the same name, and even Stillwater from Cameron Crowe's 2000 beloved *Almost Famous.*

Shall I go on?

Yet just because this elaborate, cinematic rock 'n' roll creation has been critically feted as a classic bit of Americana doesn't mean that moviegoing audiences actually made the film a box office hit when it played briefly in theaters in 1984. A historical irony is that *This Is Spinal Tap*, so widely popular today, grossed only a meager $4.5 million theatrically on a budget of somewhere between $2 million and $2.5 million. That's not exactly an earth-shattering figure.

The film did ascend to several critics' "top ten" lists back in 1984, including Roger Ebert's, Rick Lyman's, and Joe Baltake's at *The Philadelphia Daily News*. But general audiences stayed away, perhaps because—quite simply—they didn't understand what the film was about.

For example, *Forbes Magazine*'s movie critic awarded *This Is Spinal Tap* only an average rating of "C" and noted that he hadn't realized until it was two-thirds over that it was a spoof, not a real documentary.

Time magazine called the film "bizarre and desperate" in its March 5, 1984, issue: "For all its japes and jokes, the movie is really about exhaustion of the spirit: sitting in a bleak hotel suite at 4 a.m. with the bad taste of last night in the mouth and the feeling that tomorrow will not be a better day. *Spinal Tap* has as many laughs as any rock burlesque but underneath that rock it plays likes *Scenes from a Marriage* translated from the Gibberish."[5]

On one occasion, our country's paper of record, *The New York Times*, even described *Spinal Tap* as the "heavy metal joke" that "not everyone got."[6]

That descriptor alludes to the fact that some confused theatergoers may have wondered if Spinal Tap was a real band. Or as Archer Winsten suggested, "some [audiences] might believe they're watching the real thing. Only rock fans can fully appreciate the quality of the send-up."[7] And yep, that's what happened.

"Some people thought that we had discovered a real rock band, and they didn't understand why we'd make a whole documentary on a bad band," Rob Reiner reported in the *Boston Globe* on May 3, 1984.[8] Others told Reiner, with sympathy, that they loved his film, but they just wished he'd picked a more well-known subject in the genre.

"People were saying, 'Who is this band?' and 'How come we haven't heard of them?'" actress June Chadwick, Jeanine Pettibone in the film, explained during an extensive interview I conducted with her for my book, *Best in Show: The Films of Christopher Guest and Company* (Applause, 2004).

"I thought 'These guys stink; what's the big deal[?]'" admitted *The News-Star*'s entertainment columnist, Fred Phillips, in an appreciative piece called "After 20 Years, *Spinal Tap* Still Rocks."[9]

"*Spinal Tap* never really had much of a life in theaters, originally," confirms Kent Beyda, who coedited the film with Kim Secrist and supervising editor Robert Leighton and who over the years has cut Hollywood films as diverse as *Fright Night* (1985), *Scooby-Doo* (2002), and *Jonah Hex* (2010). "I don't know who had really heard of it."

"I can remember going to the premiere," recalls actress Gloria Gifford (*California Suite* [1978], *48 HRS.* [1982]), who portrayed the airport security screener who discovers the—*ahem*—artificial package nestled in bassist Derek Smalls' (Shearer's) trousers: a bulging cucumber (or was it a zucchini?) wrapped in aluminum foil. "I remember that no one thought it was that funny. It was not that successful. It made *nothing*."

Rereading these critiques and comments today, one can detect that more than a few questions about the film's premise and modus operandi were posed back in the halcyon days of Rubik's Cubes, Smurfs, bandannas, flip-up collars, preppie Izod shirts, and Sony Walkmans. And indeed, as an intrepid teenager of that era, I actually asked them myself, at least initially, just as journalist Phillips did.

I totally missed *This Is Spinal Tap*'s brief engagement in theaters, and so—like many fifteen-year-olds of Generation X—was first exposed to the life-changing message of Tap through the wonders of the then-new medium of VHS videocassettes, specifically a "home video rental" from a neighborhood shop called Currys near Brookdale Park in my home state of New Jersey.

I remember watching the film for the first time with my skeptical parents and nonplussed sister during an otherwise routine Saturday evening. As it started, I experienced five or so minutes of utter confusion before finally realizing—via the charming lyrics to "Big Bottom" (which includes the immortal line "How can I leave this behind?")—that it was all a put-up job, a carefully crafted, utterly deadpan con. My resistance quickly melted, and I was swept away by the film's good humor. My parents felt the same way, but my sister didn't quite get the joke.

I suspect this very experience was repeated in suburban households across a wide swath of the nation (and perhaps the world). Thus *Spinal Tap*, like other eighties video rental hits such as Sam Raimi's *The Evil Dead* (1983), is one of those special films whose legend grew—then exploded—through word of mouth, as well as via endless repeat rentals enjoyed in your parents' basement.

The appeal of *This Is Spinal Tap*?

Well, you figured out the joke for yourself, and so you were automatically smarter (and yes, *cooler*) than all those people who believed that it was actually "real." Nothing was spoon-fed to audiences in *This Is Spinal Tap*. The movie respected our intelligence, or at least assumed it existed. Such was not always the case with typical Hollywood product of the day.

But again, not only were some viewers apparently uncertain whether the featured band was authentic, they weren't certain what, precisely, the film was satirizing. The nuances of the closely observed documentary approach made the movie seem perhaps *too* true to life. Originally shot in 16 mm, the film was blown up to 35 mm to further augment and heighten this sense of documentary-like realism.

"At the time, it was *too close*," agrees Gloria Gifford. "It was the eighties and heavy metal rock was happening, and *Spinal Tap* was too close to itself. It was a parody of what was happening right that second, and people didn't think it was funny.

"It took a few minutes, but then that kind of rock [music] disappeared, and was no longer," Gifford continues. "Then rock music moved from Mötley Crüe and Poison and went into the grungelike phase, where people didn't dress up and didn't put makeup on. They didn't wear hot-pink pants, and they didn't use fire and smoke like Kiss did. When they moved out of that, there was *nostalgia* for when people made rock 'n' roll a spectacle."

And perhaps it was in that moment, Gifford considers, that the legend of *This Is Spinal Tap* began in earnest.

Since *Spinal Tap* originally satirized a facet of the culture that was contemporaneous, not all the jokes were immediately apparent (such as the ridiculous wardrobe and hairstyles). Some jokes had to germinate, had to wait for the culture to catch up and gain a sense of historical perspective about itself.

And because the film's dedicated creators sought to blend reality and fantasy thoroughly, the humor was never going to appeal to those who laughed easily and thoughtlessly—and on cue—at the latest Hollywood product. Rather, *This Is Spinal Tap*'s humor was carefully and wittily observed and crafted, built on foundations of intense research. *Tap* didn't offer the typical comedy drumbeat of gag after gag. It was its own thing: lethally smart and wickedly funny.

Sure, the imaginary band *really* consisted of three musically inclined comedians, but muddying the waters about that fact, these talents conducted many press interviews and promotions for their film totally *in character* . . . as Nigel Tufnel, David St. Hubbins, and Derek Smalls, the "actual" band members.

The Boston Globe piece "Exclusive!!! Spinal Tap Debunks Rockumentary" by journalist Michael Blowen, printed on July 5, 1984, is a prime example of this approach, cleverly furthering the movie's central joke by commenting on the fictional Tap's spat with auteur Marti Di Bergi (who was also a fictional creation) over the documentary movie's final cut.

"That's what really upsets us," David St. Hubbins (Michael McKean) is quoted as saying, in reference to audience perception that the band members are stupid. "We all read and there wasn't one mention of our intellectual pursuits. . . . I just read an article in a scientific magazine that claims that mildew and mold are the most intelligent forms on the planet."[10] However, not everyone was in on this ongoing joke, let alone aware of it, in 1984.

"All I know is that I was duped," declares Joe Franklin, TV and radio's famous and adored King of Nostalgia, who at the time of *This Is Spinal Tap*'s release hosted a popular late-night TV show on WWOR Channel 9 in New York.

Franklin had *Spinal Tap* booked on his show as a real band. And he didn't realize that he was being conned about the group's nature until it was far too late. He didn't see that the heavy-metal hair band sitting before him on his studio furniture was really a cadre of talented pranksters.

Nor did another guest that evening, Bruce Logan, the publisher of *TV Shopper*. He obligingly asked the "members of the band" question after question about their background, childhood experiences, and careers. This attention just encouraged the troika to continue, unabated, the undercover gag.

"*I was duped*," Joe Franklin reiterates for dramatic effect. "I was *framed*. They came on my show as a regular group, and only later on did I find out the truth. It was one of maybe four times in my life that it happened." And Franklin wasn't particularly pleased about this. "I was taken. I was really humiliated, but later on, when I became part of the joke, then I was happy."

Why the change of heart about it?

"I'm now part of a great urban legend," he notes with good humor. He sees the memorable encounter with Spinal Tap as another rich element of his five-decade-long career tapestry.

"Do you remember a group called the J. Giles Band? They were in town for one day in 1983, and their one dream was to appear on *The Joe Franklin Show*," Franklin recalls. "David Letterman offered them $75,000 for that one day, and they wouldn't do it; they came on my show. That was one of my highlights.

"That . . . *and Spinal Tap*.

"You know, I've had on five U.S. presidents and Cary Grant," Franklin continues. "I had Charlie Chaplin, and I even had John Wayne . . . but Spinal Tap is one of my all-time highlight shows based on the fact that I was very happily duped."

Over the years, a legion of new fans has also come to agree with Joe Franklin's affectionate opinion. Like the members of the band, who ultimately saw their failing musical careers resurrected (at least briefly) by sudden popularity in the Far East, *This Is Spinal Tap* took on an increasingly profitable life of its own over the years.

Impressively, *This Is Spinal Tap* has continued gaining devoted adherents with the advent of each new home entertainment format and system, from Criterion Laserdisc to CD-ROM to DVD to Blu Ray. Despite its inauspicious beginnings in movie houses, it's effectively become the rock 'n' roll movie that just won't die. Today, the movie strides atop the apex of American comedy, rock 'n' roll, and film cultdom. Unbowed. Unbroken. Unbeaten.

Perhaps even unnatural too. . . .

But how was *This Is Spinal Tap* created in the first place? How was a production so far ahead of its time conceived? And from what serious film traditions did *Spinal Tap* actually arise?

Let's "tap" into that very history here. To quote somebody much more famous than I, "Rock on!"

CHAPTER 2

Here's the Story
The '82 American Tour and the Players

As all obsessive Tapheads (or Tappers) are no doubt aware, *This Is Spinal Tap* (ostensibly a film by TV commercial director Marti Di Bergi, the guy who turned down *On Golden Pond: 3-D*) is indeed a "rockumentary," that notorious subgenre that *The Boston Globe*'s James Parker labels a "bastard form,"[1] one that is "half promo" and "half expose."

Others have described the mock-doc format (now a staple on network television) as one that lets the humor emerge "organically" and fosters a "real life atmosphere."[2]

Thus *This Is Spinal Tap* serves as an hour-by-hour, day-by-day "documentary" chronicle (in the direct cinema, cinema verité school) of the English heavy metal band

Spinal Tap's disastrous North American tour of 1982, their first such venture "across the pond" since 1977.

Promoted, or rather, underpromoted in conjunction with the release of their new album, *Smell the Glove* from Polymer Records (headed by Sir Denis Eton-Hogg), the concert tour takes the addled band members from Fidelity Hall in Philadelphia to Vandermint Auditorium in Chapel Hill to Cleveland, Ohio and California . . . and finally far astray, to Japan.

Yet while the events at accident-prone concerts and performances of nonhits such as "Big Bottom," "Hellhole," and "Stonehenge" are zealously captured by Di Bergi's roving, ubiquitous camera, so are the behind-the-scenes trials and tribulations of the brain trust composed of lead guitarist Nigel Tufnel (Christopher Guest), lead singer David St. Hubbins (Michael McKean), and bass player Derek Smalls (Harry Shearer). One such problem: Kmart doesn't wish to stock the new album because the proposed cover (of a nude woman down on all fours) is deemed sexist.

Making matters worse, the arrival of David's opinionated girlfriend, Jeanine Pettibone (June Chadwick), throws a monkey wrench into the band's delicately calibrated fire-and-ice (and lukewarm water) chemistry, causing a row at a recording studio and a squabble at a performance at a U.S. Air Force base during an "At Ease" weekend.

A brief breakup occurs when Nigel quits Tap in a fit, but the sensitive, contemplative artist ultimately returns for a triumphant encore in Japan, where the single "Sex Farm" has inexplicably rocketed up the charts to number 5. . . .

This Is Spinal Tap (1984)

CAST

Christopher Guest (Nigel Tufnel); Michael McKean (David St. Hubbins); Harry Shearer (Derek Smalls); Rob Reiner (Marti Di Bergi); Ed Begley Jr. (John "Stumpy" Pepys); Paul Benedict (Hotel Clerk); June Chadwick (Jeanine Pettibone); Billy Crystal (Morty the Mime); Fran Drescher (Bobbi Flekman); Tony Hendra (Ian Faith); Howard Hesseman (Duke Fame); Anjelica Huston (Polly Deutsch); David Kaff (Viv Savage); Bruno Kirby (Tommy Pischedda); Patrick Macnee (Sir Denis Eton-Hogg); R. J. Parnell (Mick Shrimpton); Paul Shaffer (Artie Fufkin); Paul Shortino (Duke Fame); Fred Willard (Lieutenant Hookstratten).

CREW

Embassy Pictures Presents *This Is Spinal Tap*. *Supervising Film Editor:* Robert Leighton; *Film Editors:* Kent Beyda, Kim Secrist; *Production Designer:* Bryan Jones; *Cinematography:* Peter Smokler; *Producer:* Karen Murphy; *Screenplay by:* Christopher Guest, Michael McKean, Harry Shearer, Rob Reiner; *Music and lyrics:* Christopher Guest, Michael McKean, Harry Shearer, Rob Reiner; *Music performed by:* Christopher Guest, Michael McKean, Harry Shearer, R. J. Parnell, David Kaff; *Directed by:* Rob Reiner. *M.P.A.A. Rating:* R. *Running time:* 82 minutes.

CHAPTER 3

The New Originals
The Making of the Movie (and Unmaking of the Band)

Any history of *This Is Spinal Tap* must surely begin with that troupe of four remarkably talented and dedicated actors who created it, but the film's unique energy and vibe also sprang from a comic philosophy that arose in a specific context: America in the Watergate era of the early 1970s.

Old ideas were being evaluated and discarded at a prodigious rate, turned over for something new and fresh. The war in Vietnam had undercut the long-standing idea of blind nationalism and patriotism and been judged an unjust conflict by a vocal and politically active younger generation. To boot, the ethical scandals of Richard Nixon while in office severely eroded the foundation of American trust in government. Meanwhile, an energy crisis loomed and inflation rose, threatening Americans' standard of living.

It was a turbulent, even shocking era, and everything—including how comedians judged their country and the world—was changing rapidly. A new paradigm was in the offing.

Harry Shearer (b. 1943), host of *Le Show*, later a regular voice artist on *The Simpsons* (beginning in 1990) and a contemporary political blogger at *The Huffington Post*, was paying close attention. A former child star who had appeared in such films as *Abbott and Costello Go to Mars* (1953) and *The Robe* (1953), Shearer has described his philosophy on the matter of humor as "comedy is good, reality is better." His cohort Christopher Guest (b. 1948)'s oft-stated corollary on the same matter is that comedy equals "reality" plus "one step further."

But their common approach is grounded in the 1970s. It depends on the utter believability and observations of the real actions and reactions of people . . . not ridiculous Hollywood flights of fancy, not slapstick. Not easy jokes about bodily functions.

When I conducted research for my monograph on the films of Christopher Guest, *Best in Show: The Films of Christopher Guest and Company*, I asked Shearer (in a telephone interview conducted on Wednesday, January 22, 2004) to go into a little more detail about his philosophy of comedy, and he replied, tersely: "I kind of put it in those terms because it seemed to me it [an explanation] didn't require any more length than that."

He's right, it's self-explanatory. But what Mr. Shearer kindly did next for me was describe the context of his early career, and how he came to his realization about observational, human comedy.

A political science major at UCLA and then a Harvard grad student, Shearer once worked a stint as a journalist with *Newsweek* magazine. This opportunity gave him an up-close-and-personal peek at the news, the news business, and more significantly, the political figures driving it. In many cases, he discovered, these emperors wore no clothes.

That thought no doubt remained with Shearer as he transitioned from journalism into comedy, particularly radio comedy. He became a founding member of a comedy troupe called the Credibility Gap, along with fellow future Tapper Michael McKean, David Lander (Squiggy on the popular sitcom *Laverne & Shirley* [1976–83]), and Richard Beebe. McKean, whom Shearer first met in February 1970, described Shearer as "impressive" and "eloquent."[1]

Together, this talented triumvirate starred in a successful radio show on KRLA in Los Angeles. The Credibility Gap not only played comedy clubs like the Troubador and The Giant Pickle Barrel but also released a number of profitable record albums, including *A Great Gift Idea* (1974) and *The Bronze Age of Radio* (1977). With their deadpan sense of humor, the troupe soon debated everything from bad drivers to killer bees.

But the group became famous, at least to some degree, for roasting and satirizing current events and contemporary players, including everyone's favorite—and eminently deserving—target of the day, President Richard Nixon.

"We did a lot of Nixon sketches," Shearer recalls, "and a lot of people were doing Nixon sketches in those days, and we kind of talked about it one day. And the group just didn't think that a lot of the people who were doing 'Wow, wouldn't it be wild if Nixon got high?'—those kind of 'what if' sketches—were very funny or interesting. We were trying to do what was really going on."[2]

To make a blunt analogy, the Credibility Gap's news-based, satirical brand of humor was a pioneering, prehistoric version of Jon Stewart's popular late-night program on Comedy Central, *The Daily Show*, or Steven Colbert's *Colbert Report*.

Shearer also worked with comic filmmaker Albert Brooks on an early mockumentary entitled *Real Life* (1979). It was the very first documentary, or pseudo-documentary, that Shearer was involved with, and therefore an early connection to the format of his most famous film.

"I watched the people that I worked with and admired, like Albert Brooks in the old days. He was very disciplined and once in a while you could maybe call him jokey, but his comedy came out of something very real," Shearer told me. "Or Richard Pryor. He got laughs from his heart attack.

"To me, I find that what you believe evolves, and you discover what it is by how you make your choices, and you have a moment where you realize, *Okay, this is why I do that.*"

Importantly, around this time in the seventies, Harry Shearer also commenced his long-standing hobby of collecting nonaired video of people "just sort of being in strange situations," and observing their behavior—"real," natural behavior.

"That makes me laugh a lot more than, you know, 'the cop is a Martian and the deputy is an alien and the kid is a dog!' sort of stuff. 'Isn't that wild?' All that hokey stuff."

This hobby led Shearer to understand how reality could be far funnier than any slickly manufactured comedy. In particular, he sought to vet observational-based humor at a time when many more mainstream comics were doggedly sticking to what he terms "fish out of water" scenarios.

"Now, there are situations where people find themselves in new circumstances," Shearer adds, "so I can't say that there are no fish out of water situations, but the ones in movies outnumber the ones in real life by about five thousand to one.

"To me, nothing is funnier than humans, and the way we actually behave. And you don't need to dress it up or extend with a lot of imaginative flights. You just need to be a good observer. And that's the toughest thing, apparently. Because people find it much easier to go into a room and talk about or sell things that are 'what ifs' rather than get real comedy out of how people really are."

Embracing this philosophy of humor, Shearer, McKean, and the Credibility Gap reigned at the vanguard of a new style of comedy in the early 1970s, and this style would eventually come to inform and shape *Spinal Tap*.

At the same time on the left coast, an impressive and serious young fellow, a graduate of New York City's High School of Music and Arts and Bard College named Christopher Guest, was simultaneously honing his skills as a talented mimic and comic. Already a friend of McKean's (they had met at school in the late 1960s) and a talented musician who had jammed and performed with Arlo Guthrie for a time, Guest began his stint with *National Lampoon* in the early 1970s.

Guest was a featured player on *The National Lampoon Radio Hour* and memorably appeared in a significant off-Broadway theatrical production entitled *National Lampoon's Lemmings*, which opened January 25, 1973, and ran for 350 performances.

The comical musical revue was set at the fictional "Woodchuck Festival," a free concert of "peace, love . . . and death." The setting may have been pure *Woodstock* (1970), but the title *Lemmings* came from a cryptic comment made by rock music icon Mick Jagger in the altogether disturbing rock documentary, *Gimme Shelter* (1970), about the disastrous Altamont concert of 1969 (where there had been at least one death in the audience): "They're like the lemmings of the sea."

In *Lemmings*, the refrain was, "The man next to you is your dinner." This was either a warning that a celebratory atmosphere at overpopulated concerts could turn disastrous on a dime (like Altamont), or a hippie commentary about not wasting valuable resources.

Guest's costars in this unusual venture included future *Saturday Night Live* stars Chevy Chase and John Belushi and *Grease*'s (1978) Rizzo herself, Stockard Channing. Co-directed by Tony Hendra (who eventually portrayed Spinal Tap's manager, Ian Faith) and Sean Kelly, *Lemmings* was a loosely structured intertwining of contemporary music and outrageous comedy. Belushi parodied Joe Cocker, Chevy Chase took on John Denver ("Colorado"), and Guest mimicked James Taylor with the song "Highway Toes," which featured the lyrics, "Farewell to Carolina/Where I left my frontal lobe."

Guest also parodied brilliant but pretentious Bob Dylan with the tune "Positively Wall Street." Guest sang, and the composition featured Dylan's trademark harmonica and cryptic language. Specifically, the unrepentant Dylan-like singer suggests you don't look to him for answers. Or wisdom, actually.

With Kelly and Hendra, Guest also coauthored the tune "Pizza Man" and Alice Playten's "Golden Oldie," which parodied Shangri-La's famous 1960s biker anthem, "Leader of the Pack"—only the chorus sounds like people spasming, and the singer thinks of her boyfriend, Johnny, every time she orders a pizza (because he ended up looking like pizza after a road accident).

Following *Lemmings*, Guest segued to television and earned an Emmy for his writing on the variety show *The Lily Tomlin Special* (1975). He also guest-starred on a popular TV series and cause célèbre of the disco decade, CBS's fiery domestic sitcom, *All in the Family* (1971–79). It starred the late Carroll O'Connor as the bigoted, blue-collar Archie Bunker from Queens, New York, and a very young, very intense Rob Reiner as his liberal Polish son-in-law and intellectual nemesis, Mike "Meathead" Stivic. Guest appeared in a flashback episode involving Mike's first date with Archie's daughter, Gloria (Sally Struthers). He played Mike's college roommate, and you'd be really hard-pressed today to recognize him.

The son of comedy legend Carl Reiner, Rob Reiner likewise brought a potent bag of tricks to the creative foundations of *This Is Spinal Tap*. In addition to his experience with a sitcom like *All in the Family*—which was far more realistic and courageous in its approach to comedy material than most network sitcom programming of the epoch—the two-time Emmy winner was a founding member of the improvisational comedy group at UCLA called The Session. Then, for a time, he joined another comic squad, The Committee. Before essaying the popular role of Meathead, Reiner brought his considerable writing chops to politically minded TV shows such as *The Smothers Brothers Comedy Hour* (1967–69).

So if you're inclined to play the always-rewarding "Six Degrees of *This Is Spinal Tap*" game, you might just detect the nexus by which all of these artists came to work together on the film. Rob Reiner was married for a time to Penny Marshall, star of *Laverne & Shirley*. A regular costar on her show was Michael McKean, playing the scatterbrained character Lenny (of Lenny and Squiggy fame). And McKean had already worked with Shearer in the Credibility Gap.

Meanwhile, Christopher Guest knew Reiner from his *All in the Family* appearance and had actually worked with McKean, his old friend, on a professional basis for the first time on a project also related to the *Happy Days* (1974–84) spin-off: the *Lenny and the Squigtones* album, released by Casablanca Records in 1979, which asked the immortal question, "Is the world ready for Squigtomania?" The album, a parody of late sixties rock, featured such songs as side A's "Creature Without a Head" and "Love Is a Terrible Thing" and side B's "Only Women Cry," "Honor Farm," and "So's Your Old Testament." More significantly to Tapheads, this rare (and now valuable) LP represented the first "appearance" of a strange British guitarist called Nigel Tufnel. That moniker is reputedly based on the name Eric Clapton.

Finally, it wasn't until the ABC skit program *The T.V. Show,* directed by Tom Trbovich, that all four of these talents united onscreen and Spinal Tap was truly conceived. Although *The T.V. Show* was envisioned as a satire of the late night *Midnight Special* (1973–81) and other clichéd TV efforts of the day, the project also heralded the first joint appearance of Tap, as Shearer, Guest, and McKean played members of a very bad, "hopeless"[2] rock 'n' roll band from the UK. The first song the band ever performed was called "Rock 'n' Roll Nightmare."

During the making of the pilot, Guest apparently slipped into the character of Nigel Tufnel—which he had reputedly been developing for ten years—several times between shots. Harry Shearer told *The Village Voice's* Peter Orchiogrosso in March 1984 that he, Guest, and McKean began ad-libbing their characters right there on set too, while waiting for a cranky fog machine to operate correctly.

Written by Tom Leopold, Phil Mishkin, and Martin Mull, and shot by acclaimed cinematographer Stephen H. Burum (director of photography to Brian De Palma on films including *Carlito's Way* [1993] and *Mission: Impossible* [1996]), the Harry Shearer-produced *The T.V. Show* filled a ninety-minute time slot when it aired on June 24, 1979, but the ratings were not stellar.

This era represented the height of "skit" programming popularity (following *Saturday Night Live*'s pop culture ascent), and ventures such as *Fridays* (1980–82), starring Michael Richards; *The New Show* (1984), starring Buck Henry, John Candy, and Jeff Goldblum; and, sadly, *The T.V. Show* didn't stand out to audiences. Even though the Shearer satire never made it beyond pilot stage, something wonderful nonetheless arose from the experience: at long last, Spinal Tap—or as it was originally known, Spynal Tap—had arrived.

The band would rise again in a few years, but in the meantime, Reiner cowrote and starred in a TV movie that aired on February 2, 1982: *Million Dollar Infield*. He appeared in the telefilm (about Long Island residents on a local softball team) with future Tap cast members Christopher Guest and Bruno Kirby.

Docudrama: Form Is Content

The other important story behind the parturition of *This Is Spinal Tap* doesn't involve its four intrepid progenitors, but rather an entire school of film and filmmaking. The late sixties and early seventies had witnessed a revolution, or a "new freedom," in filmmaking technique with the advent of cinema verité, also known sometimes as direct cinema.

This "new wave" of nonfiction filmmaking, spurred by the recent availability and affordability of lightweight equipment, stressed the unmanaged (or rather, undirected) filming of real folks, and the spontaneous and "as live" sense of a viewer "being there." It also involved the utilization of portable, easy-to-manage equipment; the recording of sound "live" on location; and the primacy of cutting over long-take filming, meaning that the narrative would be shaped after production, in the editing bay.

Perhaps most importantly, the old model and tradition of nonfiction, documentary filmmaking (which included a script and usually an elaborate form of narration) was entirely rejected in an all-encompassing effort to create for viewers a "model of reality" that, according to scholar Richard Barsam in his 1973 text, *Non-Fiction Films: A Critical History*, included "many types of ambiguity."[3]

Barsam further notes that films of this type served as "creative treatments of actuality," taking their subjects from the "raw" and making them, eventually, seem "more real" than the "acted article" forged in the traditional filmmaking process.[4]

This fascinating new approach was ultimately utilized at the height of rock 'n' roll music's second coming, during the sexual revolution days of the 1960s, in films such as Michael Wadleigh's *Woodstock* (1970), the Maysles' *Gimme Shelter* (1970), and Baird Bryant and Johanna Demetrakas's *Celebration at Big Sur* (1971). In some of these, rockers like Keith Richards or Mick Jagger were thus seen for the first time not from the canned and filtered perspective one might expect for a "star," but—importantly—as they truly were, moment to moment, without rehearsal or pretense.

Interestingly, this new format revealed not just outstanding concert performances and brilliant musical talent but also pomposity, confusion, and a general fogginess on the part of some highly admired rock icons. Circular logic reigned, and overinflated egotism was the order of the day.

More than that, however, the form of the new documentary revealed how a canned idea (that Altamont was going to be "the greatest party of 1969") could suddenly and inextricably give way to messy reality.

"We all thought we were going to do another Woodstock," Peter Smokler, *This Is Spinal Tap*'s director of production and a cameraman at Altamont, told me. "We thought it was going to be a huge human document we would chronicle. The culture was still there, and it was really cool that the time wasn't over yet. But when we got there it was just this big dusty bowl. It wasn't a pleasant circumstance, even if there wasn't rain and mud. It was and hot and dry, and there were Hell's Angels everywhere and that's not always a fun mood to be around. They're a little scary."[5]

So cinema verité was truly a warts-and-all proposition. Indeed, this is why so many young directors preferred the form. It promised unpredictability.

And for those captured prominently onscreen in such films, there was no place to hide, no safe harbor. The D. A. Pennebaker cinema verité *Dont Look Back* (1967) provides another perfect example of this. The film's subject, Bob Dylan, clashes with the press during his London adventure and is revealed to be short-tempered. He even seems to boast a cruel streak as he puts down a young man interviewing him, a sincere science student, for a wince-inducing five minutes. It's just . . . mean.

Dont Look Back also reveals subtly how Dylan feels threatened and jealous of a competitor, Donovan, but the film ultimately emerges as an even-handed portrayal of the icon. Dylan's musical ability and talent shine through all, but that doesn't mean the guy wasn't also a son of a bitch (at least during the making of the film).

And it is this important idea that proves the critical element of the form, the one that *This Is Spinal Tap* ultimately exploited so adeptly. Cinema verité-style realism gave the filmmakers the incredible opportunity to chart the very same fine line as these classic rock documentaries: between stupid and clever, between canned and spontaneous. Hagiography was out; authentically observed "human colors" were in. Through this format, the creators of *Spinal Tap* would speak most trenchantly about music, musicians, rock history, and their times.

"We knew we were making it in a documentary style," Shearer told me. "So we were making fun of a band and of the adoring documentarian simultaneously."

Just Begin Again: *Spinal Tap* Rises and Falls

Charting the rise and fall of an unlucky, untalented English rock band and determining the right onscreen method to present it were only the initial steps in conceiving a full-fledged feature film.

At one point early in *This Is Spinal Tap*'s development, there was some discussion about shifting the focus of the drama to the band's "roadies," some "backstage Rosencrantz and Guildenstern angle," according to Shearer. But that idea was dropped when the creators realized that the band itself was "instrinsically more interesting, and funnier." Finally, the group settled on an a very specific brand of English rock band, one that had lived through many musical "incarnations" together in nearly two decades, and would thus be the correct age to be portrayed realistically by Guest, Shearer, and McKean.

It was soon decided that Reiner would not actually be in the band, the director once reported, because he didn't look good in spandex. Instead, he would play the film's director and narrator. The Scorsese model in *The Last Waltz* was something the band members were aware of and "certainly taking into account," according to Shearer.

This opened up a new focus of the satire. Scorsese—for all his obvious gifts as a talented filmmaker—never seemed in *The Last Waltz* to ask probing questions of his subjects, and furthermore seemed bound and determined to contextualize the rockers as deities, and his effort to document them as a quest seeking "rock heroes in the Olympian mode."[6] In *The Last Waltz,* Scorsese could be seen rehearsing and re-shooting questions, not to mention buddying around with his subjects.

This kind of mock profundity and self-awareness (or lack of self-awareness) was just begging to be skewered, and with Marti Di Bergi, *Spinal Tap* happily obliged. Reiner, in the tradition of Scorsese, would even don a cap (of the naval vessel *Coral Sea*) for the film.

Another one of the overarching themes of *This Is Spinal Tap* would be a critique of eighties rock 'n' roll music itself. The film was crafted during the last days of what Shearer calls "The roller-coaster ride that started in the late sixties where rock 'n' roll was supposed to be this big social force, and by the time we made *Tap* that had been clearly played out, but people were still walking around posing as if it were true. To me, that was part of the thematic thrust of the movie: the music has left the building."

Another element of *This Is Spinal Tap* that was never altered: Shearer, Guest, and McKean would do all their own singing and playing. The initial impulse for that was the troika's shared frustration that in all the rock 'n' roll movies they watched, the actors kept getting it wrong.

"Actors were supposedly playing guitars with their fingers in impossible positions, given what they were hearing," Shearer explains. "Forty million people in this country have taken guitar lessons, so why would you insult the audience quite that gratuitously if you don't have to?"

Regarding the music, Shearer also notes that "it's something we enjoy doing, and if you can do it, why not do it? There are a lot of different stories to tell, but we're able to tell stories about these people because we can deliver the goods in terms of that aspect of their lives. I think as actors, we can connect with these characters because even though they're very different people from us and make wildly different choices than we would make, we do relate to the weirdly twisted passion that they have. Because it's one that we share.

"As actors, it does give us a leg up in portraying these people," he adds. "That's a very different relationship to the characters, I guess, than what you have if you can't do it."

Even before a coherent story line was fashioned, all the actors had to formulate a basic "fund of knowledge," a shared twenty-year history of the fictional band that they would all agree upon, and more importantly, draw upon for the spontaneous interviews and other critical scenes.

This exhaustive history (going back to the year 1964, when Nigel and David were but wee lads) was referred to as "the Bible" for *Spinal Tap*, and took the group's performers from the era of hippies to the heyday of head-bangers. It focused on what gigs the group performed where and what incidents occurred at each show. For instance, one gig took place on the mythical "Isle of Lucy," a verbal joke about the series, *I Love Lucy* (1951–57). And Spinal Tap, the world would soon learn, had suffered through a whopping thirty-seven personnel changes over the years (the majority of them involving ill-fated drummers).

Reiner, McKean, Shearer, and Guest also had to compose—and the band had to learn and rehearse—several original Tap tunes, ones that sounded authentic to the genres and time periods during which they were crafted. And the whole rock scene in general also had to be carefully observed, understood, and then synthesized with comedic overtones.

On the former front, the fledgling Tap joined together to write eleven such pieces, with titles like "Heavy Duty," "Tonight I'm Gonna Rock You (Tonight)," "Big Bottom," "Rock and Roll Creation," and "Hellhole."

And on the latter front, this new "fictional" band even began accepting real gigs at clubs in Los Angeles and Anaheim. They opened for a number of rock bands throughout California, including the uniquely named Killer Pussy, and were mistaken for a real band by the audiences time and time again.

Much as their movie would later be mistaken for a real documentary. . . .

Guest, McKean, Reiner, and Shearer also did other homework. They attended concerts by AC/DC, Judas Priest, Mötley Crüe, and Saxon to augment their knowledge base. They sought out and screened every rockumentary they could get their hands on, from the aforementioned *The Last Waltz* to the production that reportedly was most difficult (and tedious) for them to get through, Ernest Day's Led Zeppelin pic, *The Song Remains the Same* (1976). That documentary was a filmed record of Zeppelin's 1973 *Houses of the Holy* tour, specifically a concert at Madison Square Garden, but the movie was saddled with bizarre dream and hallucination sequences (replete with gangsters, knights, and other colorful characters).

All of this background detail, study, and research ultimately paid off in a number of ways. For instance, in one memorable scene, Tap discusses with Marti Di Bergi the genealogy of the group. First it was known as the Creatures, then the Originals, then the New Originals, then the Thamesmen, and finally—for the ages—as Spinal Tap.

This moment is an eerie echo, one might note, of a sequence in Scorsese's *The Last Waltz*, when The Band contemplates its labyrinthian and storied heritage as the Crackers, then the Honkies, before settling on the generic The Band. But more importantly, the members of Spinal Tap *didn't know when, how, or even if* Reiner would ask about the band's history and lineage. They knew nothing about his questions in advance (an effort to foster spontaneity), yet they all had to be working on the same page so as to interact in what appeared to be a "truthful" manner.

Pound Notes, Loose Change, Bad Checks: Funding *This Is Spinal Tap*

The hard work and careful preparation to make *This Is Spinal Tap* an accurate and hilarious reflection of contemporary rockdom was laudable, but as the originators of the material soon learned, that didn't mean the movie was going to prove an easy sell.

Why? Well, Rob Reiner remained untried, never having directed a feature film before. And the three actors portraying the band members weren't exactly household names. Worse, they were Americans attempting British accents. Or at least two of the three were: Guest actually boasts British heritage and title as an English lord.

But regardless, the whole "direct cinema," documentary-style approach was another stumbling block, no doubt confusing many a prospective studio head. If they couldn't understand the film's premise and central joke, what were general audiences to make of it?

The first film executive who detected the potential in *This Is Spinal Tap* was wily Lord Lew Grade, a wildly successful businessman who had seen many hits over the years on British television with such ventures as Patrick McGoohan's enigmatic paean to individual liberty, *The Prisoner* (1967), and Gerry and Sylvia Anderson's lavishly produced and trippy outer-space adventure starring Martin Landau and Barbara Bain, *Space: 1999* (1975–77).

The head of Incorporated Television Company, Grade sought to repeat his small-screen success at the international box office as the seventies became the eighties. In fact, there was no third season of the popular *Space: 1999*, according to star Landau, because of Grade's new emphasis on movies, in particular a $35 million adaptation of the Clive Cussler espionage best-seller, *Raise the Titanic* (1980). Marble Arch, the U.S. arm of Sir Grade's global entertainment empire, liked the idea of *Spinal Tap* enough to commit seed money to the project, and Martin Starger (*Saturn 3* [1980]) was assigned as project producer.

The four talents behind the project were supposed to take that seed money—$60,000, according to Karl French in *This Is Spinal Tap: The Official Companion*[7]—and pen a traditionally structured, industry-standard screenplay.

Shearer, Reiner, McKean, and Guest happily accepted the dough, sequestered themselves in a hotel room, and began pounding out a screenplay. But it didn't take many hours at a typewriter before they realized that this idea simply wasn't working in a conventional narrative form and that the script could not accomplish its stated goal: explaining what the movie was about and basically selling it to the money men. Then they hit on the notion that would be much better (and far more effective as a sales strategy): they would craft a twenty-minute "demo reel" of the project as they intended it.

"My understanding is that Sir Lew Grade of Marble Arch had hired Rob Reiner to write this movie and had given him [approximately] $50,000," reports cinematographer Peter Smokler.

"We got a deal to write a script about this band, and sat in a hotel room for about three or four days with me typing, to actually write a first-draft screenplay," Shearer confirms. "Then at one point we looked at each other and said, 'You know, this is supposed to be a sales tool, getting this movie made, and nobody is going to be able to read this and understand what we mean. This won't help us get the movie made. We don't need the money, we're all kind of okay right now, why don't we take this money and instead make a demo?'"

Rob Reiner then went back to the financiers and said, "'We're not going to write this, because all these guys are improvisational actors and they've been doing these bits for years and years, and they're just ready to go. So we're just going to make it and not write it,'" relates Smokler. "But they insisted on him writing it."

The group of four decided to make the demo anyway. They set about assembling their minimovie, called *Spinal Tap—The Final Tour*, with producer Karen Murphy (*True Stories* [1986], *Drugstore Cowboy* [1989], *Magic in the Water* [1995]). This demo was shot in a scant four days, and it was at this point that Smokler, a veteran documentary cameraman on such films as *Gimme Shelter* and *Jimi Plays Berkeley* (1971), entered the picture.

Smokler had just completed a long and exhausting shoot on a cinema verité-style documentary project focusing on

Warner Earhart and E.S.T. (Earhart Seminar Training), a prominent and popular self-realization phenomenon of the disco decade that was heralded for its supposedly "modern" and "scientific" approach to personal improvement. Take the training and it changes you, supposedly enabling you to handle all of the problems in your life.

"It was a really weird phenomenon," Smokler remembers. "We never bought into it, as a film crew."

Though the Earhart film was supposed to be transformational and transcendent, it turned out to be a flop, lasting in theaters for a scant weekend. However, working on the project granted Smokler precisely the type of experience he could put to good use on *This Is Spinal Tap*.

"I came into this thing [*Tap*] really knowing my methodology for observational filmmaking," the director of photography elaborates. "This guy who was with me on E.S.T., Hubert Smith, was a fanatic about cinema verité style, and I ended up with a 35 mm print of the film."

That print would turn out to be quite useful as a calling card.

"They [Rob Reiner and Karen Murphy] started looking for a cameraman, and they don't know where they got my name," Smokler continues. "Karen Murphy still doesn't remember where they got it. So anyway, I went in there and

I took a 35 mm reel from the Earhart movie. I guess a lot of other guys came in with tapes, and I don't know what kind of projects they were, but mine was a pure verité project: I didn't know who was talking [in the shooting of the film], and I never directed anybody to do anything.

"So I found a reel that was really emotional and I said, 'Well, I can show this to you in the theater, and it looks exactly like what your movie will look like projected: same camera, same kind of stock,' and we went to a screening room at CBS [Studio City] on Radford.

"So I showed them this reel in the theater, and Rob got really excited and started jumping up and down. 'Did you tell him what to do?! Did you tell him to do that?! This is exactly what we're looking for!' It was that kind of moment.

"So I got the job to shoot the twenty-minute piece—and they were all really funny in the presentation—and then my understanding is that once we shot it, Marble Arch folded."

Indeed, Marble Arch was in no condition to respond to the gang's opus either positively or negatively. The aforementioned *Raise the Titanic* and another costly release, *The Legend of the Lone Ranger* (1981), proved to be critical and box office bombs. *Raise the Titanic* grossed only $8 million on its budget of over $35 million, and *Legend of the Lone Ranger* grossed $8 million on a budget of $18 million. Thus the studio—and Lord Grade's master plan for global silver screen dominance—went under faster than, well, the *Titanic* itself.

Now evicted, the Spinal Tap brain trust had to worry about funding their project again.

"The whole project died," Smokler recalls.

Fortunately, everybody involved in *Spinal Tap* stayed in communication with one another and directed their energies toward other collaborations.

"The group of us—meaning Harry, Chris Guest, and Michael McKean—we started making a bunch of little things for a cable company," Smokler explains. "It was called *Likely Stories* [1981]."

Unfortunately, this obscure TV series, a collection of comedy short tales, is unavailable today on VHS and DVD, so the Tap collector is out of luck. But Smokler does remember many of the details behind it.

"Christopher Guest did a Dashiell Hammett-type show where he played all the roles. It was a Phillip Marlowe thing shot in black and white, and Christopher Guest played the detective, the secretary, and this Indian thug. He played the old man who knew the real story, he played the widow, and he played a cadaver. It was great.

"They each directed one," Smokler clarifies. "Harry directed one about the making of an industrial film. It was literally behind the scenes of an industrial film, and Michael

McKean was the celebrity spokesman . . . saying how much he loved the people who worked at this company, which was really funny."

Perhaps, at least so far as *Spinal Tap* lore is concerned, the most significant of these *Likely Stories* contributions starred Bruno Kirby, playing the very character he would eventually portray in the film.

"Another of the films we did for *Likely Stories* was 'The Tommy Pischedda Story,'" Smokler reveals. "It was an expansion of his character as the limo driver. It was based on some guy who lives in an apartment in the middle of Hollywood who owns every Sinatra album . . . unopened. He must have had two or three hundred albums in that place, and we shot it in his apartment. It was a little story about Bruno as the chauffeur, and there was a love story."

Meanwhile, *This Is Spinal Tap* still struggled to come to full term. At one point, United Artists picked up the option to develop and fund the film, at least for a while. But before anything more could happen, MGM bought the company and new executives, including David Begelman, came in. Consequently, interest in the project evaporated and *This Is Spinal Tap* was dropped a second time, consigned to development hell.

Matters looked downright grim for "the world's loudest band" until Norman Lear—the producer of *All in the Family* and a longtime friend of Reiner—made the four guys an offer they couldn't refuse. His new company, Embassy, recently purchased by his highly successful TV company, Tandem Enterprises, would produce the film at a cost of a little over $2 million. Lindsay Doran suggested the meet-up and team-up, and it was a deal.

"We all got back together again," Smokler recalls, "having done our little projects here and there."

But that doesn't mean the travails were over.

From Script to Stage: Building a Better Tap

Dated September 10, 1982, and credited to Christopher Guest, Michael McKean, Rob Reiner, and Harry Shearer at Spinal Tap Productions in Studio City, the script for *This Is Spinal Tap* is called, simply, *Spinal Tap*. It is a scant fifty-nine pages in length, and contains only two instances of specific dialogue, in particular director Marty Di Broma's opening and closing narrations, which diagram the band's tale of "rock and roll survival." This shooting script follows the general narrative arc of the completed film, though with some notable differences between page and screen.

Marti Di Broma would eventually be renamed Di Bergi, and some of his early pontifications in the opening narration (on whether his rockumentary is a "microcosm," "macrocosm," or "minicosm") didn't survive that translation.

Later, after an argument over who is the "hottest" guitarist in England (David or Nigel) one Tap fan boasts that David has autographed her diaphragm. This material also did not survive to final cut.

Some stagecraft details are different in the shooting script as well. For example, a sizable mirror is wheeled onstage at one venue for a performance of "Tonight I'm Gonna Rock You (Tonight)," in order to show off the band's "cretinous" attempt at June Taylor Dancers–style choreography.[8]

Later, at the tour kickoff party at Parallel Records (rather than the movie's Polymer Records), some "powdered refreshment"—cocaine—is served by Bobbi Flekman (Drescher), a surprising, even revelatory touch that didn't make it into the film, and brings up an interesting point. The audience never actually sees the band partaking of illegal drugs in *This Is Spinal Tap*, though drug use is certainly an important (and destructive) element of the rock scene. From the general fogginess and demeanor of the band, drug use may simply be assumed, but it was likely a good move not to picture it in the final cut. The image of Tap members snorting lines of coke might have seriously damaged the sense of the group's naïveté or amiability.

Also present in the shooting script is a bizarre encounter with a groupie who loses a contact lens, only to remember that she has inserted two in the same eye, and a very funny subplot featuring a personality called Stellazine, lead singer of an opening act called the Dose. The source for the "in-flammatory" lip sores seen in the final cut, Stellazine is described, amusingly, as a younger, punker, sexier, and "better" Deborah Harry. And apparently, she has had her way with each member of the group.

Another change involves a deleted musical number. In the script, a picturesque tour through Washington, D.C. spurs an inspired Nigel to create a patriotic, enthusiastic American anthem called "King of the [*sic*] America." This song is performed to Marty Di Broma's "cinematic meditation" montage of national monuments including the Lincoln Memorial, the White House, and the Washington Monument. Before long, however, things degenerate and the band is seen at less-inspiring locales: a car wash, a miniature golf course, the candy aisle of a supermarket, and a field with cows grazing in it.

Some other scenes in the script also didn't make it to the screen. A heavy chandelier falls on drummer Mick during a performance of "Heavy Duty" at Vandermint, NC, and in Chicago a rendition of the song "Short and Sweet" turns anything but as the band's instruments strike a note and simply won't stop striking it. While that note sustains (and sustains . . .), all the performers glumly leave the stage, save for Mick, who takes this unexpected opportunity to solo on drums.[9]

Perhaps the most startling change from script to film involves the introduction of David's sullen teenage son, Jordan. He's an American punk-rocker type, and the freewheeling David is surprisingly disapproving of him, wondering why Jordan can't grow hair like a man. This is an interesting subplot because it exposes the persistent generation gap, even in personalities we assume would be open-minded and accepting, like rock stars. But the introduction of David's son (from his first marriage) also makes David seem less sympathetic. His arrested development and bad behavior seem less amusing when a child, and unhappy one at that, is introduced into the proceedings.

Another moment that Tap fans would surely have loved to see play out onscreen but only appears in the shooting script involves Derek forcing his groupies and bandmates to endure a Betamax showing of his cheapo Italian movie, *Roma '79* (directed by Marco Zamboni), in which he plays a "futuristic villain."[10] Think *The Tenth Victim* (1965).

Now that sounds classic . . . and also true to rock history, considering how rock stars have, over the years, flirted with making movies that aren't particularly good—like David Bowie in the fantasy *Labyrinth* (1986), or Mick Jagger in the sci-fi actioner *Freejack* (1991), and so on.

Other changes from the script appear largely cosmetic. In it, Artie Fufkin is called Artie Katkavicz, and he cracks a soft-boiled egg over his head, an even more humiliating act than his famous "kick me in the ass" routine in the film.

Finally, the film's script closes with a wraparound, book-end narration not included in the final cut. In it, Di Broma characterizes Spinal Tap's duration on the public stage as something akin to being broken down on the side of the road, waiting for fifteen years for the Auto Club to arrive.

Back in Harness: Principal Photography

This Is Spinal Tap began production in spring 1982, with cinematographer Peter Smokler behind the camera and Reiner at the helm. Smokler worked diligently on the project to capture what *Magill's Cinema Annual 1985* came to praise as a "witty" presentation of "the grainy visual style of *cinema verité*."[11]

Smokler was assisted in this mission by concert lighting designer Richard Ocean, who had designed shows for the Stray Cats and Boston, among other chart-toppers.

Joining the movie's primary cast for the quick shoot were several notable actors, including Billy Crystal (as a mime waiter); Patrick Macnee—John Steed of *The Avengers* (1961-1969) fame—as Sir Denis Eton-Hogg; a very young, pre-*Nanny* Fran Drescher as Polymer representative Bobbi Flekman; and *National Lampoon* editor Tony Hendra (who reportedly once considered becoming a Benedictine monk) as duplicitous manager Ian Faith.

Fresh from *Likely Stories,* Bruno Kirby played Tommy, a limo driver with a big thing for Frank Sinatra (an autobiographical touch on the actor's part) who warned Di Bergi that Spinal Tap and metal music were just "fads." John Huston's daughter Angelica Huston essayed the role of the befuddled, literal-minded prop designer responsible for creating an underwhelming piece used in the band's big number, "Stonehenge."

Fred Willard, who would later become a star of Christopher Guest's documentary-style comedies in the 1990s (*Waiting for Guffman* [1997], *Best in Show* [2000], and *A Mighty Wind* [2003]) also teamed up with the cast as Lieutenant Bob Hookstratten, a straitlaced officer who would escort the band to their gig at a western Air Force base, a sequence based on a real-life event involving Uriah Heep and John Sinclair, Tap's keyboardist for the twenty-minute demo. (And by the by, this incident has also been claimed as a "real" event by artists such as R.E.M. and Black Sabbath.) Willard had first met Reiner while he starred in a series *Fernwood 2 Night* (1977), being shot in the same studio as *All in the Family.*

"I had met Rob Reiner because I was doing *Fernwood 2 Night* in the same studio where he was doing *All in the*

Family, and we would pass each other," Willard told me. "I also worked with his then-wife, Penny Marshall, on *Laverne & Shirley*, where Michael McKean and David Lander were. And I had great respect for them, so I had a feeling when a part came up in *Spinal Tap* that it was Harry Shearer and Michael McKean that said, 'You've got to get Fred Willard for this.' Now, I may be wrong. . . ."

Willard also was acquainted with Christopher Guest, though he didn't remember that at the time. They had both been in the cast of a 1970 off-Broadway theatrical production of Jules Feiffer's *Little Murders.*

"We did *Little Murders* in New York," Willard told me. "Christopher Guest was an understudy in the play, and I think I met him—I have a vague memory of him. I know his mother was a casting woman, and I don't think that I was ever actually onstage with him. He reminded me of it years later."

Given his familiarity with the members of the band as well as his impeccable comic timing, Willard was a natural for the part in *Spinal Tap*. Although he was reluctant to take the role of what he calls "another jackass," when asked to meet with Rob Reiner about his heavy metal movie, he quickly reconsidered. What changed his mind? He watched the twenty-minute demo reel while McKean, Shearer, Reiner, and Guest were out on a coffee break, and couldn't believe that what he had seen was improvisation rather than an authentic documentary.

As it turns out, Willard had already been rather enamored with the notion of a production that appeared real but wasn't, as he told me during our interview for *Best in Show*.

"That kind of documentary style has always fascinated me. When I first came out to Hollywood, there was a show called *Divorce Court*. I would watch it during the day, and I would say, 'Is this real or not real?' Because they didn't *seem* to be like actors," he recalls. "And then suddenly, one day, I noticed an actress being a little bit dramatic, and I said, 'Oh, actors,' but something was very realistic about this. And what it was is that they used real lawyers to plead the cases."

With his background in improvisation, Willard knew immediately that he wanted to appear in *This Is Spinal Tap*, and when the creators of the film returned from that coffee break, he told them he didn't even care about money or billing. He just wanted to participate.

Another critical role in the film was that of Jeanine Pettibone, David's meddling, strangely garbed, and rather troublesome girlfriend, ultimately the cause of the band's schism during the waning days of its American tour. Taking on this character was actress June Chadwick, who came aboard late in the film's development process, leaving a martial arts movie entitled *Revenge of the Ninja*. She had been practicing her limited martial arts repertoire, but the movie kept changing locations and start dates, so she "slid sidewise, and I hope upwards, to be in *This Is Spinal Tap*."

"They had apparently done this twenty-minute demo of it," Chadwick recalls, "and were taking it around and showing it to people. And the consensus, they thought, was that there was no story line to it, and they needed a story line. So they came up with the story line of my character coming in. . . ."

Chadwick remembers being called in for the audition, and then being asked back to improvise with Guest, McKean, and Shearer. She was skeptical that Americans could pull off a cockney accent, but was surprised and delighted by the cleverness, dedication, and good humor of the ensemble.

"We just sat around improvising," she says, "and it was fun, and I had a good time, and that was really it."

Later, Chadwick had a hand in fashioning her own character's memorable sense of style (or lack thereof). "I considered myself quite trendy at the time. London was well ahead of L.A., and still is, and has always been a little avant-garde in its fashion, if you can put it that way," she reports. "So a lot of the clothes were actually mine, but they were put together all wrong. What *wouldn't* go with what, and then put it in there, and add something frightful to that too. And

I was having such fun with that it was one of those things I decided looked really cool."

Gloria Gifford, who had recently starred in the Rick Rosenthal horror film sequel, *Halloween II* (with Christopher Guest's future wife, Jamie Lee Curtis), remembers how she came aboard the project.

"Well, I had done a movie with David Steinberg, who is now [in 2004] a big director of *Mad About You*, and he directs *Will & Grace,* and all those things. He was a comedian in the 1960s, from Canada, so he was friends with John Candy and all those folks like that. That comedy world is very cliquish.

"So I did this comedy with John Candy called *Going Berserk* [1983], and David Steinberg was the director, and I just loved him," Gifford continues. "We worked together again on another project, and by then he was good friends with Christopher Guest and those guys. They were looking for people who could be funny for *Spinal Tap,* and he recommended me to them."

An audition was scheduled with due haste.

"I went in and I met with Christopher Guest and Michael McKean, and they really liked me and they told me, 'Okay, you're going to go back and meet Rob, because he's really the director,'" Gifford recalls.

But if meeting the band had seemed easy, she was about to encounter a roadblock with Di Bergi.

"I went to meet Rob, and Rob looked at me—*and he was very dismissive*—and he said, 'I'm not looking for a Vogue model.' He said it right with me in the room."

Gifford was taken aback by the director's blunt remark, but stood her ground and got it together.

"I looked at him, and I said—very quickly, because I'd been doing a lot of movies with improv, and I was quick on my feet—'Does this character wear pants?' And he said, 'Yeah.' And I said, 'You know that bulge around your waist when your pants are too tight?' And he said, 'Yeah.' And I said, 'I can get that for you.' And he just looked at me and said 'Okay,' and I left."

The disappointed actress assumed that this was the end of her association with the picture, but not so fast.

"About half an hour later, I called my manager and I said, 'Oh my god, he hated me,' and she said, 'No, he *hired* you,'" Gifford remembers. "He showed me no warmth whatsoever."

Still, Gifford bears no hard feelings about the interview. "I went to a revival of *This Is Spinal Tap* with Rob [in 2000], and I chatted with him, and I don't think he even remembers how it happened."

Others in the cast of *This Is Spinal Tap* included Not-Guffman himself, Paul Benedict; David Letterman sidekick

Paul Shaffer; future *Wayne's World* (1992) star Dana Carvey as Crystal's partner in mime; and *St. Elsewhere* (1982–88) cast member Ed Begley Jr. Each of these performers, along with the main dramatis personae, was responsible for creating the specifics of their characters . . . but without the aid of dialogue.

Perhaps the most impressive aspect of *Spinal Tap* is that virtually *all* the dialogue featured in the film was improvised. For the specifics of each scene, original and realistic dialogue had to be created. And it had to be funny. But not falsely so—and that was the most devilish detail of all.

Tapped Out? Improvising a Masterpiece

For some in *Spinal Tap*'s cast, the prospect of rampant improvisation, which expert Michael McKean has termed "an arcane art," was utterly terrifying. For others, it was merely a matter of applying training and patience. Rob Reiner graciously allowed the cast to view the film's dailies, and for many of the performers, this was a heaven-sent opportunity to see how they were doing and to calibrate their performance.

June Chadwick found the dailies particularly helpful; Fred Willard, in contrast, never particularly enjoyed seeing them, because he always felt he could do better.

"If anything, it was like, *Oh, I don't need to see much more than that*," Chadwick recalls of her reaction. "Because

I thought, *It works.* If I hadn't seen them, I might have been much more paranoid.

"I think comedy is difficult anyway," the actress reflects. "If you have a script and you know what's going to happen, that's scary too. Because you rehearse the thing and everybody's laughing, then you come to shoot it and there's dead silence. It just isn't funny. Everyone's quiet, no one's laughing.

"It's kind of the same thing with the improv we were doing. I think I really didn't know I was being funny, necessarily. What I tried to do was say things that I thought might be ridiculous, but I did want to be real. I really wanted to *believe* what I was saying. That's as far as I got. I didn't get into, *I want to be funny.* Trying to be funny would lose the funny. It's the fact that you don't know that you're funny that makes it funny.

"I never liked clowns when I was little. Why, when they have a whole arena, do they have to go step in the frigging bucket of paint? And if somebody's made a nice cake, why do they have to shove it in somebody's face? That isn't funny to me. What's funny—and maybe this is a British thing—is the verbal humor."

Chadwick also recalls that Reiner was a very good director, and more importantly, a good director for *her.*

"It was easier than it might have been because Rob told me to shut up," she recalls. "So I thought, *That saved me!* He was very good on that [the movie] in terms of me squeezing my way in [into the band] incrementally. So if I said too much initially, it would be too much too soon. So I was quite happy to sort of shut up. But the problem with that is that everyone else was so damned funny.

"If you know your character well, the improv is great," Chadwick says. "You have to react in character. You can't plan what you are going to say. You can have an idea of things that, if you can fit them in . . . you'll fit them in. But that doesn't always happen."

Chadwick's introduction to the film also happened to be Jeanine's first scene, the moment in the film wherein a groggy Spinal Tap is onstage performing a sound check in early afternoon, having just awakened from a late night of debauchery. The first copies of the *Smell the Glove* album cover arrive in a brown box. Of course, there is no cover art: the album is merely . . . *black.*

For Chadwick, this was a particularly difficult sequence because of its sustained length, because it was her first, and because it just grew funnier and funnier as the members of Tap passed the black album (a riff on the Beatles' famous *White Album*) from one to the other and commented on it.

"It was one of those things that starts out sort of a little bit funny, and it just frigging builds and builds until it was more and more ridiculous. And nobody really came up with saying anything about this . . . it [the black album] was just sort of too stunning. I remember at that point I really thought I was going to lose it, so I thought of my school or my education that was just horrible, so I could literally take my mind absolutely out of the scene and not listen. Because if I had listened, I think I would have gone. And nothing can be repeated."

Laughter was also a concern of Peter Smokler, from behind the eyepiece.

"It was hard to hold the camera sometimes, because I was laughing," he reveals. "Actually, I got referred to a yoga teacher who taught me how to 'breathe through laughter' so I wouldn't be ruining shots."

Gloria Gifford remembers her time actually shooting *Spinal Tap* as not particularly funny, but something of a whirlwind instead.

"On the day that I went to shoot *Spinal Tap*, I thought I would bring a little wig, because my own hair is very long . . . I have, like, Indian hair," she begins. "I brought a wig so I could look more African American. I walked up and said [to Reiner], 'You want me to wear this?' and he said, 'Yeah, sure—fine.' And I went into make-up and then I came out.

"We were at the airport, and Rob said, 'Okay, well, uh, this is the scene,' and he described it. He said [to Gifford] that 'there's just one line you have to say. And the rest is improv.' So we did it, and maybe we did two takes.

"And he said, 'Fine, cut.'"

And that was that.

"And I was driving home at 10:30 in the morning thinking, *Did I just do a movie?*" Gifford recollects. "Because I've never been in a movie in my life that you arrived at, then . . . came home [from] in an hour and a half. It was *that* fast, because it was improvised. They hired a lot of improvisational actors."

Wanting to know more, I asked Gifford if she knew that Shearer would be brandishing a rather large cucumber in his drawers . . . one wrapped in tinfoil.

"They did tell me that," Gifford acknowledges. "Rob just said, 'There will be . . . something you'll see,' and I said, 'Okay.'"

And what was going through Gifford's mind when she did the scene with Shearer? "I just wanted to be bored; bored with him [Derek, not Shearer]; bored with the job, and then suspicious of him and that was it. I just made my own choices; there was really no direction."

The idea, as in all cinema verité films, was to allow the moment to happen and let the camera capture it *while* it was happening. Life unfolding, happening before our very eyes, apparently unstaged and almost "as live," is a critical aspect of the film's unique tapestry.

The danger inherent in this approach was that the film seemed so real, so truthful, that some viewers might mistake it for truth, not comedy.

"None of it lets you know that this is a spoof," Smokler considers. "But when you see a bunch of midgets dancing around a stone, you've got to know what's going on. When a character says, 'You can't dust for vomit,' . . . I mean, it's really a testimony to how thick people are.

"Rob was quoted in *Entertainment Weekly*—it was the issue with *King Kong* on the cover [November 18, 2005]," says Smokler. "They talk about his career, and he attributes a quote to me that I don't remember, but I do remember a number of times saying to him, 'I'm not sure people are going to get this joke.'

"He'd just say, 'Don't worry, this is a fifth-viewing joke.'"

In addition to the improvisation, there were some rehearsals for the most important scenes. Chadwick remembers rehearsing the so-called "Doubly" scene in the café, for instance. "And the reason we had the rehearsal was because there were points that had to be put in there," she explains. "And the problem with improvising is that when you get people that aren't necessarily able to do it very well, everybody wants to talk, and everybody wants to talk on top of each other. And I think it was smart of Rob to say, 'Let's rehearse this so we know where the attention needs to be.' It was probably as much for the cameraman as it was for us too.

"I was a bit clueless myself as to everything that was going on, and how it was all going to be put together," she further relates. "We had a script and we followed it, according to the script. There wasn't really much in the script to go on. There was a basic story, going from A to B, but no dialogue. I was given the fact that I was into horoscopes and yoga, or something.

"And for the horoscopes, I got some books and basically learned things all wrong if I could, you know. You know, Saturn's in the third house of the sixth moon or something. I had no idea what I was talking about and I thought that was probably a good thing. . . . You don't ever play stupid, but ignorant."

It was in the rehearsed café scene that Chadwick's most famous line, the mispronunciation "Doubly" (as opposed to the correct "Dolby") was discovered.

"That line was given to me by Chris Guest, and I thank him profusely for it each time I see him," Chadwick told me. "No, I don't, but he very graciously said, 'It's the way you executed it that was funny.' Again, it was one of those things that once I was given it, there was no question that 'doubly' was the right phrase to use. So it was a combination of both of us, I suppose."

Peter Smokler recalls that shooting many of the film's now-trademark scenes was a challenge. For instance, the long tracking shot involving the band getting lost backstage was a bear from a logistical standpoint.

"There was no dialogue in the script, so that tracking scene was tough because it was very confined . . . so you had to sort of calculate the areas where they [the cast] could possibly go, and then light those areas. . . . The thing about the way the film was shot, you never really knew where they [the actors] were going to go, or what they were going to do. . . . [Originally] it was a much, much longer sequence.

"Almost every take was totally different than every other take, dialoguewise and blockingwise," Smokler explains, and so his training in the documentary framework really came in handy.

"That's what they were looking for, someone who could really make that work. If you see a shot in the film that's coming into focus, for instance, it wasn't planned. It was that I was zooming in to get focus on a new person, and that's the way you do a documentary. Essentially, it *was* a real documentary."

Making matters more challenging, throughout the majority of the shoot, Smokler was limited to a single camera.

Other cameras were brought in only for the concert performances. The most on hand—ever—was three.

"When we did the concerts, we brought in two more cameras," he describes. "We had a guy on the dolly in the audience, and we had another hand-held guy. H. J. Brown and Ric Robertson . . . they were two really good documentary cameramen, who actually started [in the business] before me, and I always thought it would be great if I could hire them. H. J. was my hero. The same with Ric.

"When we had H. J. there for a concert venue, if we did a dialogue scene at the same time, we could use two cameras since we had them there. For instance, the scene when Christopher Guest comes back and announces Japan wants them to tour . . . we had two cameras for that scene, but everything else was one. I think that was the only dialogue scene we had two cameras for."

The most difficult part of filming the concert scenes was not performance (which was mimicked through playback of studio-recorded material), but managing the minimal number of extras populating the stadiums. Lest we forget, *This Is Spinal Tap* was a very low-budget feature, and this means that it was not feasible to pack the large venues with hordes of screaming fans.

"We had to think of the audience being there. So the dolly shot from the audience, I think, was shot from the balcony . . . and we'd put a row [of concertgoers] in front of the cameraman," says Smokler. "And then we'd block everything with them so you couldn't see that there were only four rows of people in front of the stage. The rest of the hall was empty.

"Even the comeback concert in Japan . . . we only had a couple of rows down the stage, and people up in the balcony."

As a film journalist, I just had to know: did anything horrible or untoward happen on the set of *Spinal Tap*? Smokler describes the movie as a fun and happy shoot, but talk of the Japanese venue does spark a particular memory.

"That was a nasty story. We had to reshoot that, because the extras person didn't hire any Japanese people. They were all Filipino or Chicano or something like that. So we went to dailies and Rob said, 'These people aren't Japanese! What's going on here?'

"And then I remember the next morning, the unit manager got really mad at me, because it was his extras guy. And I just said, 'All I do is shoot them!' I mean, there were a few Japanese people, but they were very old and they were sitting in their chairs. We had to redo all that because we needed Japanese faces with fists in the air."

Finally, after thirty days and nights of filming in locations meant to represent eighteen different cities and countries,

TOP: Filmmaker Marti Di Bergi (Rob Reiner) prepares a probing question for the heavy metal rockers of Spinal Tap.

BOTTOM: Projecting Power: Spinal Tap in action. Left to right: David St. Hubbins, Mick Shrimpton, Nigel Tufnel, Viv Savage, and Derek Smalls.

Icons of Rock Legend (and Myth?): David St. Hubbins (Michael McKean, above) and Nigel Tufnel (Christopher Guest, below).

Hot and Cold: Derek Smalls (Harry Shearer, above) and Jeanine Pettibone (June Chadwick, below).

Of Great Historical Significance. Spinal Tap in the "Flower People" Epoch (above) and in the Age of Heavy Metal (below).

Stagecraft 101: Nigel Tufnel solos (above), and Derek Smalls is about to step into an embryonic disaster (below).

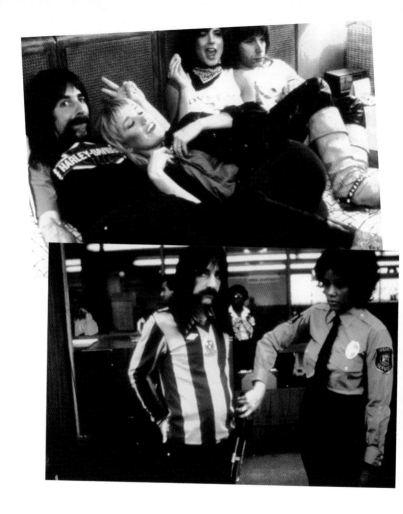

The Tao of Derek Smalls. Derek relaxes with groupies (above) and is waylaid by an airport security screener (Gloria Gifford, below), who suspects that he isn't exactly projecting power in his trousers.

TOP: Happy Days: The band at Castle Tufnel.

BOTTOM: Spinal Tap signs a record deal with Polymer Records.

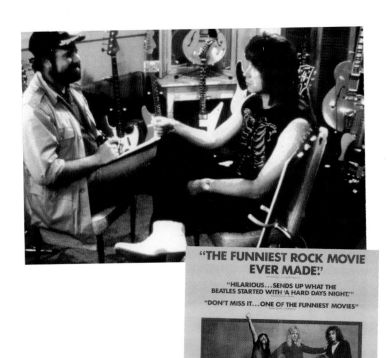

TOP: Marti Di Bergi (Rob Reiner, left) questions Nigel Tufnel (Christopher Guest, right).

BOTTOM: The publicity poster for *This Is Spinal Tap* goes to eleven.

with more than ten original songs in the mix, *This Is Spinal Tap* completed principal photography.

Although Rob Reiner also confided in Richard Harrington at *The Washington Post* that "there were a lot of fights that went on" while making *Spinal Tap*, including scenes with cast members screaming, storming out of rooms, and returning, perhaps the greatest challenge on the film was yet to be faced: *cutting*.

Now was finally time to review the raw footage and begin shaping what would one day become a modern masterpiece of the absurd.

Making a Big Thing of It: Editing *This Is Spinal Tap*

This Is Spinal Tap was fashioned as though a real documentary. That means a veritable ton of footage shot (actually fifty hours in all), usually in long-shot mode. And a laborious editing process (by some accounts six months, by some eight) would necessarily follow the shooting schedule.

Kent Beyda, who had served as an assistant editor with Joe Dante and others on Allan Arkush's cult classic, *Rock 'n' Roll High School* (1979), joined the project after Kim Secrist, supervising editor Leighton, and Rob Reiner had commenced the cutting process and discovered it was a long, hard slog.

When he arrived at the *Spinal Tap* offices, Beyda had just finished working on another rock film starring Malcolm McDowell as a character named Reggie Wanker.

"I came on [*Spinal Tap*] after they'd finished shooting, actually, because they realized they had so much material to deal with, and they needed some help. I had done *Rock 'n' Roll High School*, and I was actually doing this other movie that Allan Arkush directed at the time, called *Get Crazy* [1983], which is a very funny movie that is based on his experiences. I think it's a lost movie. It sort of fell between the cracks.

"But I had done a bunch of music videos as well, so I went in to interview with Rob and got the job and started immediately," Beyda recalls. "My first job was cutting the number for 'Hellhole.' I sat down to cut it on Monday afternoon, and that evening I told everybody I was ready to show it, and they said, 'What?' And they said, 'You have a cut on it?!' because it had taken them a week to cut the musical numbers. So they were flabbergasted I had done it so quickly, and we looked at it, and it was good . . . and it just kind of evolved from there."

The project was different from a typical or conventional Hollywood film, Beyda recalls, because he had to find clever places to slide in the necessary cuts between takes. The footage had been shot in a number of very long sequences, with long takes, but as a comedy, the movie had to move at a fast clip and preferably be under an hour and a half in length.

"It was basically, you know, there was a script, but it was just an outline," Beyda describes. "They would do the scene, and then revise it and do it again. They would do it maybe two or three times in long takes. So we had these really long takes that we would cut up, and try to make it work by cutting away and stealing things to be able to bridge between one take and the next.

"It's a different approach," he says. "It was more fun, really. It was kind of hard to go wrong because there was so much good stuff.

"We looked at our first cut about a month later, which was like six or six-and-a-half hours," Beyda remembers, though some sources have tabbed it at being closer to four. The thought of a six-hour or even four-hour version of *This Is Spinal Tap* is certain to make dedicated fans drool, and according to Beyda, the film actually worked remarkably well at that elephantine running time.

"We sat down at this dumpy screening room in Hollywood and we ordered Chinese food and just watched the whole thing for hours. It was quite something," he remembers. "It was an epic. It was fantastic. It was a really good movie. It was full of all kinds of currents and eddies and subplots and characters . . . all of which got dropped in the final eighty-five-minute version."

And what was the template for deciding what would stay and what would go in the film?

"As with any comedy, what happens is that you have to get it down to the story," Beyda emphasizes. "What's the story about? What's the trajectory of the story? That was the process there.

"There was plenty of hilarious stuff that didn't fit with the story of the movie, and it went right away," he acknowledges. "Basically, what happened is that we had a wall with file cards on it, and each card had a scene written on it, and after we'd look at the movie, we'd gather round and look at the file cards.

"We'd all look at one scene and someone would step up and take a card off the wall. And everyone else would go, 'No, really?' So then we'd shuffle the cards around and discuss different configurations and different ways of doing it.

"Rob Reiner, even though he was a first-time director, was very good about letting things go," Beyda notes. "In fact, he was more eager to drop things than I was, oftentimes. We got into fights about losing certain things, but it was quite a creative process. The editors and Rob and the three guys—the band—all participated in that process."

And knowing that there was so much deleted footage, one just has to wonder what treasures were buried. Even though deleted scenes have appeared on laserdisc and DVD versions of the film over the years (including a bootleg longer version), surely there are gems that have never been seen, just waiting to be excavated for an "ultimate edition" Blu Ray?

"So much great stuff is not in the movie," Smokler laments.

"There was a great sequence at the recording studio where things had really gone sour, and it was a very serious scene that added to the whole trajectory of the characters, that made it that much deeper," Beyda recollects.

"There's also a part where Jeanine finds a younger replacement for Nigel to play with the group [and] there was jealousy [from David] for this young guy," says Smokler

"[And] Cherie Currie was in the movie playing the lead singer of a band called the Dose," Beyda adds. "That whole subplot was cut out of the movie."

"She was from the Runaways," Smokler details. "And [in the movie] Spinal Tap comes into a venue and their opening act is already onstage and they're called the Dose. She [Currie] is in a skin-tight, blue lame outfit, and she's absolutely gorgeous. And they stop and look up at her and say, 'We've got to tour with the Dose.'"

"She's then seen with each band member," elaborates the cinematographer, "but the *previous* member has a cold sore on his lip. And so she's with all of them, except the drummer, and then the band manager [Ian] comes in and says, 'We need to have an emergency band meeting.' They get together, and you have four faces in the band covered with cold sores, except the drummer. And they all say, 'We've got to get rid of the Dose.' And the drummer says, 'What's wrong with the Dose?'"

Alas, Cherie Currie's scenes are no longer in the film. "I don't even think she's seen. You might see her once in one of the limo rides," Smokler suggests. "She also had a song in the movie too, called 'Video Games.' It was a long, long, droning song that just went 'video *games*,' 'video *games*,' 'video *games*,' . . . on and on. That's all it was."

Pared back to focus on the important elements of the story, *This Is Spinal Tap* was finally ready to be previewed. But more changes were coming.

"After we had finished the movie, we had some test screenings and they didn't go well," Kent Beyda reports. "So Rob brought me back with an assistant, and we sat down for about a week and recut the movie from top to bottom, and we put in a couple of songs that had been taken out. We reshuffled it a bit and refocused it based on the audience reactions from the test screening. So that's something a lot of people don't know about."

Some material was dropped in this recut, and some restored. "'Heavy Duty' came back in," Beyda recalls off the top of his head. There may also have been some tweaking of the classic "Stonehenge" number, if memory serves.

"That's something I also edited," Beyda elucidates. "That was the second musical piece I cut. It was always very successful. We had different ways of getting into it, different ways of setting it up. There used to be more discussion about it. There was something about her [Huston's character] designing it, maybe even something in her studio. But it boiled down to setup and joke."

Again, Beyda credits Reiner as an exceptionally clever and canny director in his editing decisions. "The comic timing was really from Rob, because Carl is his father and he has that in his blood. He knows good comic timing, and that was a big, big plus in editing that movie."

"Editing is always the final rewrite of a movie," Harry Shearer told me. "The crucial job is how much of the storytelling you don't need. Almost always, unless you're making an incoherent big action movie, you've shot more storytelling than you need, because you're never sure that the audience can follow what you're doing. . . . There's a thing you feel in the room when the audience has been told something one more time than they need to be told. So their interest and focus momentarily flags and is withdrawn. *I know this already.*

Let's get on with it. You feel that in the room with them. So the editing process is . . . taking stuff out until you've really got the essential spine of the story and nothing more. And hopefully some laughs along the way."

When all was said and done, the cast and crew were pleased with the final cut.

"We knew that it was something special," says Beyda. "We knew that it was funny, creative, and fresh, and our main goal was to make it into a movie with some shape."

But?

"When it came out, people were totally confused by it." Beyda laughs. "A lot of people thought it was about a real band. 'Why would I want to see a movie about this band? They stink! I've never heard of 'em.' Things like that."

Well, that's nitpicking, isn't it?

"Rock and Roll Creation": *Spinal Tap* Unspooled

This Is Spinal Tap opened in select theaters across the United States in early March 1984. On a staggered schedule, it went to houses like the Nickelodeon Cinema in Boston, the K-B in Washington, D.C., the Loews New York Twin, 57th Street Playhouse, and Greenwich Playhouse, all in the Empire State.

The critical response was overwhelmingly and instantaneously positive. Writing for *Los Angeles* magazine, Merrill

Shindler called *This Is Spinal Tap* "the funniest rock movie ever made."

John Nange, critic for *Films in Review*, praised the film's sense of "wild-eyed exuberance" and remarked that "the mannerisms and affectations of rock mania have never been harpooned with such rock-bottom Pythonesque lunacy."

Writing for *The Chicago Sun-Times* on March 1, 1984, the prominent film reviewer Roger Ebert called the movie "one of the funniest, most intelligent, most original movies of the year," and opined that it "simply, slyly destroys one level of rock pomposity after another."

"I think it's one of the most brilliant films I've ever seen," adds Gloria Gifford. "When I see it, I laugh at every single actor and every single situation. I don't even have a favorite one, because they're all so funny to me."

Kent Beyda describes *This Is Spinal Tap* simply as "the gold standard" of the mockumentary form, and Peter Smokler says that only now—more than twenty years after *Spinal Tap*'s release—is he really coming to terms with his involvement in what has become a cult classic.

"It all happened slowly," he reminisces. "You know, a movie lasts in theaters maybe a maximum of five weeks . . . maybe ten. *Spinal Tap* lasted maybe two weeks in not very many theaters. But then people started hearing about it.

"As time went by, people I would see would mention it and start reciting dialogue from it. . . . I'm still just beginning to realize it," he says with a sense of awe.

"The people who know I worked on *Spinal Tap* start genuflecting when I meet them. I'm still discovering that it's a big deal."

Tap After *Tap*

In the years following *This Is Spinal Tap*, many of the players in the film made stops on *Saturday Night Live* as regulars and guests, and others dove headfirst into other movie projects.

Harry Shearer and Martin Short joined to make a quasi-documentary short film on *Saturday Night Live* about male synchronized swimmers. Meanwhile, Guest directed *The Big Picture* (1989), a movie about the movie business that featured friend and *Tap* collaborator McKean as a cinematographer.

As for Rob Reiner, he found new success at the box office with *The Princess Bride* (1987). Those with eagle eyes will notice a cameo by Marti Di Bergi's *Coral Sea* naval cap in the movie's first scene.

In 1991, Guest and McKean teamed to write and direct several episodes of a short-lived sitcom entitled *Morton & Hayes*, starring Kevin Pollak and Bob Amaral as a hapless, Abbott and Costello-style comedy duo. Each week they'd have a different-style period adventure. One was a horror pastiche, one was a film noir, and another was a Three Stooges kind of comedy. McKean guest-starred in one segment of *Morton & Hayes* entitled "The Bride of Mummula," playing the evil Dr. Mummenschwantz.

In 1992, however, Tapheads had cause to rejoice: the world's loudest band would reunite for the 25th Anniversary London Sell-Out Tour.

In other words, Spinal Tap appeared live and in concert at London's Royal Albert Hall in July 1992. The prestigious event was hosted by Bob Geldof and served as punctuation for the band's successful world tour, which included destinations like Canada and Australia. The impetus behind the tour: the release of *Break Like the Wind*, the band's new album, which ultimately climbed to number 61 on the *Billboard* album charts.

Also released at this time was "Bitch School," a new Tap music video that appeared on MTV. A TV special aired that included concert footage and even new skits that followed up on the events of the famous 1984 film. Nigel and David are depicting revisiting their childhood homes, a rundown apartment complex in Squatney. There, the duo reminisces about their poverty, and Nigel even reports how his mum fixed them "deep-fried cotton balls" for dinner on some occasions. The audience also catches up with Derek, who now toils at his father's Sani-Phone business. He has also been trying (unsuccessfully) to become a real estate mogul.

June Chadwick, Paul Shaffer, Rob Reiner, and Fred Willard all make encore appearances in character in *The Return of Spinal Tap*, and the band also encounters Mel Torme, who sings a few bars from "Big Bottom."

The latter half of the 1990s brought Christopher Guest's next mockumentary, *Waiting for Guffman* (1997), starring Fred Willard, Eugene Levy, Paul Benedict, Catherine O'Hara, Parker Posey, and Michael Hitchcock. The film concerned a community theater company in small-time Indiana, and the group's not-very-realistic aspiration to go to Broadway. Harry Shearer composed with Guest a very funny tune in the film, "Stool Boom."

In 1998 Guest, Shearer, and McKean contributed their vocal skills to the Joe Dante film *Small Soldiers.* They played action figures named, respectively, Slamfist, Punch-It, and Insaniac.

In 1999, Guest, McKean, and Shearer re-teamed as their beloved and long-established *This Is Spinal Tap* characters again, in this instance for an audacious, bravura, nonstop, eighty-five-minute running commentary on *This Is Spinal Tap* featured on the new DVD release.

In this amazing, stream-of-consciousness performance, Nigel, David, and Derek recall the making of the film, provide updates on their activities, and react to new developments in the world (including the rise of E-Bay). People whom the band members don't seem to like much are dismissed as being "dead." And Jeanine, we learn, has penned a children's book called *A Stretch Mark Named Mischa*.

Amazingly, this feature-length DVD commentary is as funny, fresh, and silly as the original movie itself, and adds a whole new layer to the film. Appropriately, the Shearer/McKean/Guest commentary won the Video Premiere Award in 2001 for Best DVD Audio Commentary. The DVD was also nominated for Best DVD Overall Supplemental Material.

Also in 2000, *This Is Spinal Tap* played again in select theaters for the first time in fifteen years. It added a considerable haul to its total box office returns, as this was the first and only opportunity for Generation Xers to see *Tap* on the big screen. Home video had for most been their first exposure to the film.

In 2003, McKean, Shearer, and Guest regrouped not as Tap, but as another band: a folk group from the 1960s with equally bad luck (and bad marketing), The Folksmen. The trio performed their hits "Wandering" and "Old Joe's Place" in the hit mockumentary, *A Mighty Wind*. Once more, the talented trio did all of their own singing and playing.

The twenty-first century has seen further Spinal Tap adventures as well. In 2007, Spinal Tap reformed to sing their new tune, "Warmer Than Hell," at the Live Earth event at Wembley Stadium sponsored by former Vice President Al Gore in an effort to spotlight the cause of global warming. Tap played there alongside Genesis, The Police, Madonna, and the Red Hot Chili Peppers. Tufnel, in typical clueless fashion, apparently believes that global warming is caused by wearing too many layers of warm clothes. He also mistook Wembley for Wimbledon.

The coup de grace in 2007, however, was a new fifteen-minute film featuring the band, introduced by Rob Reiner, in character again as Marty Di Bergi. This effort (only vaguely concerning "eco-awareness") opened the Tribeca Film Festival in New York on April 25 and was well received.

In 2009, word arrived that Spinal Tap's first new album since 1992 would be released, and that it would feature "Warmer Than Hell." The album was titled *Back from the Dead*, and also featured "Celtic Blues," a jazz odyssey, and classics such as "Big Bottom" and "Sex Farm." To celebrate their album, *This Is Spinal Tap* also made TV appearances on *Late Night with Jimmy Fallon* and the short-lived *The Tonight Show with Conan O'Brien*. This time on the late-night circuit, there was no repeat of any Joe Franklin-style hijinks.

The group also took part in an Unwigged and Unplugged Tour in 2009, at locations including Toronto's Massey Hall. This was the first time ever that Shearer, McKean, and Guest performed Tap tunes out of uniform, so to speak, without their long "heavy metal" hair.

Also anticipated at the time of this book's writing was the Spinal Tap seven-minute short, *Stonehenge: Tis a Magic Place,* featuring the band's first visit to the monument that has vexed them so considerably over the years. Hopefully, it will be a no-dwarves-allowed engagement.

Spinal Tap lives!

CHAPTER 4

Beyond Doubly
The Top Eleven Reasons *This Is Spinal Tap* Endures

After going down in flames in the nation's movie houses, *This Is Spinal Tap* returned, phoenixlike from the ashes, and ascended to a seemingly eternal pop culture afterlife. But the pertinent question to ask about the Tap phenomenon is simply: *Why?* Or in the vernacular of the band: *Huh?* Why has an eighty-two-minute mock documentary about a fake (and bad) band endured, even flourished for over twenty years?

Of course, the film is scathingly, unrelentingly funny. Don't discount that fact. There are more good jokes per minute in this lean, mean rocking machine than there are pauses in a Harold Pinter play, as the wisecrackers at *Mystery Science Theater 3000* (1988–99) might note. But let's face it: there are lots of funny movies hovering around out there in the global entertainment universe, and not every one boasts the cachet of *This Is Spinal Tap*.

It would be tempting to provide a unifying theory of *Spinal Tap*, one complete and satisfying answer that ties everything about the film's popularity together into one neat package, but the plain fact of the matter is that *This Is Spinal Tap* works so well—and remains such a good film—for a variety of reasons. So, without further ado, allow me to present the top eleven reasons *This Is Spinal Tap* survives.

1. It is true (and accurate).

Let's begin with what I call the accuracy principle. I don't want to be a buzz kill by bringing up dull concepts like homework and preparation again, but the fact is that *Spinal Tap* would not seem half as funny had the film not been so accurately observed and splendidly researched; had not Guest, McKean, Reiner, and Shearer spent so much time learning their roles and understanding the rock world.

Bill Cosford at *The Miami Herald* commented on this aspect of the production. "The details are right," he wrote, "and the performances by Americans with flawless British accents are perfect. Even the names are splendid caricatures (meet David St. Hubbins, Nigel Tufnel, Derek Smalls, Mick Shrimpton, Viv Savage, and Ian Faith)".[1]

The Boston Globe's Steve Morse agreed the film was an "uncannily accurate" view of a "business full of poseurs and cartoon characters."[2]

Many critics also saw "real life" rock incidents in those portrayed in the film, a signifier that the film hewed close to rock history. "The tragic drummers bit is reminiscent of Keith Moon and the Who, and the sexist album cover controversy points straight at the Rolling Stones," opined writer Gene Triplett.[3]

This attention to detail and rock history is evident in many aspects of the film. For example, the title, *This Is Spinal Tap*, deliberately evokes *This Is Elvis*, Malcolm Leo and Andrew Solt's 1981 cinematic ode to the King of Rock.

The *Smell the Glove* album cover debacle apparently relates to a 1979 Whitesnake album called *Lovehunter*. In that famous cover, a nude woman (viewed from the rear) is seen mounting a coiled, gigantic snake.

And when Nigel Tufnel discusses his musical trilogy in D minor, he speaks of his love of Mozart and Bach, noting that his piece is in the mode of both, a so-called "Mach" composition. This turn of phrase evokes memories of Beatle Ringo Starr and his famous line that he was neither "rocker" nor "mod," but rather a "mocker."

Jeanine's destructive role in the band's male bonding also seems a clear echo of Yoko Ono, or perhaps Anita Pallenberg, even though that wasn't necessarily the actress's intent.

"I didn't start to see anything until I had the tenth person say, 'Oh, it's a Yoko Ono character,' and I thought, *Oh, maybe it is*," recalls June Chadwick.

Nor would the film have been so strong and atmospheric an experience had cinematographer Smokler not proven so well versed in the style of cinema verité. When examining *Spinal Tap*'s popularity, all of these facets remain critically important.

Yet to enjoy *Spinal Tap*, it isn't necessary to understand that the name of mock director Marti Di Bergi is Rob Reiner's tribute to *Marti*n Scorsese of the *Last Waltz*, Steven Spielberg, Brian *Di* Palma, and a host of other young auteurs from the movie brat era in cinema history.

Nor is it necessary to realize that as the film was being made, Norman Harris of Norman's Rare Guitars loaned the production company over three dozen collector's items, which were then insured for a million dollars, including Nigel's prized Fender six-string bass.

But the upshot of this gift was that the guitars utilized in the film were accurate to each and every one of Spinal Tap's various eras, from "Flower People" in the 1960s to "Sex Farm" in the 1980s. Even the right microphones were utilized, and everything, down to the style of album covers, attempted to carefully re-create the details of rock history. As an audience, we don't smell any fakery, and that's a critical thing.

This accuracy extends to the musicians in the band, and the fact they all play their own instruments, with aplomb. Indeed, that was one of the primary reasons Guest, McKean, and Shearer wanted to make the movie in the first place, because they had all seen so many rock fantasies wherein notes on the soundtrack didn't match fingers in the frame. These glaring inaccuracies were always "enough to make you choke on your popcorn," according to Dan Forte, who wrote a piece on *Spinal Tap* for *Guitar Player* in February 1992. *Spinal Tap* was purposefully designed to be different. In Forte's words, the movie "seems more true to life than most of the actual documentaries about existing groups."

I believe that the quest for accuracy, that *This Is Spinal Tap* is "consistently convincing," in the words of *Monthly Film Bulletin*'s Kim Newman, also led to a sense of camaraderie. There are no hot dogs in the cast, nobody trying to take credit for the final shape of the film (although in 2004 there was a little dust-up between Tony Hendra and Michael McKean in *The New York Times* over creative "ownership").[4] Still, when Guest, McKean, Shearer, and Reiner lobbied the Writers Guild to include all the people involved in the creation of the film as cocreators, only to be rebuffed, it was a true and gracious acknowledgment of the fact that film is a collaborative art form.

And *Spinal Tap*, for all its big, brassy funny moments, also kowtows to reality by featuring some sense of pace and verisimilitude. There are soft, touching moments too. I always think of Derek on the phone in a hotel room, arguing with his first wife, clearly miserable. It's almost a throwaway moment, yet it feels eminently real and suggests a life for the character beyond the text of the final cut.

"A lot of people told me over the years that they thought that was a real person at the airport," Gloria Gifford says, expounding on *Spinal Tap*'s accuracy principle. "And I'd tell them 'That was me,' and they'd say, 'Really? That was you?'"

Another way of putting this is that the characters in the film seem real. "Everybody is truly a real character, they tell their story. You can almost watch it as a documentary and start out laughing," Fred Willard told me.

"It's like watching Wayne Newton explain something," he continues. "You're watching him, but you're also saying, *He's in another world here with his 500-acre ranch and 4,000 Arabian stallions and this and that*. And yet, when you watch him, he's a real person. It's not too far out. It's not an over-the-top comedy."

Research and reality precede laughs, and *Spinal Tap*'s accuracy and sense of reality actually make it funnier. We recognize the people, the situations, and the jokes as strangely realistic (and for more information, check out the next chapter about real life *Spinal Tap* moments).

Accuracy is one thing, but satire tends to be cold and distancing. The makers of *Spinal Tap* didn't want their parody to come off in that fashion, accurate to the point of cruelty. And that brings us to what I believe is the second reason for *Spinal Tap*'s longevity.

2. In a strange way, it's affectionate.

Yes, the members of the band may be thick, deluded, and hepped up on their own particular brand of Kool-Aid, but as viewers, we *like* them.

We want them to succeed, and we understand that the way they see themselves isn't exactly how they are perceived by others. Although terrible things happen to Tap (like being billed second to a puppet show), the band members remain human, likeable, and touching.

"Rarely have pretentious people been portrayed so affectionately," wrote Robert Christgao and Carola Dibbell for the *Village Voice* in March 1984.

"We see the group wither and degenerate, and somehow, even though it's all fiction, we become emotionally involved," wrote Joe Baltake in his piece "Putting on the Rockers" for the *Philadelphia Daily News*.[5]

"Comedy is really picking on people's weaknesses or peccadilloes or people's habit," Chadwick considers. "Which doesn't necessarily mean that they are bad people. . . . That's why I don't think they're [the Tap brain trust] mean spirited. I don't think my character was mean spirited."

Indeed, *This Is Spinal Tap* has a way of winning people over because of its affectionate nature. "If to know them is not precisely to love them, then at least one wishes them well as they regroup yet again for a tour of Japan," wrote Wayne Robins in his review of the film.[6]

Although reportedly rock star Sting didn't know whether to "laugh or cry" when he first saw the film, the rock world has mostly embraced *Spinal Tap*. It's not just real and true, it captures something about musicians that is a little sad and a little funny. Consequently, many rockers have proven more than willing to join the ongoing gag about Spinal Tap being a "real" band.

"Christopher Guest was part of a promo for Marshall amps when they came out with the amp that went up to twenty, several years ago," Peter Smokler recalls. "They hired him to promote the new amplifier and they brought it out at Guitar City on Sunset Boulevard. They invited all of these famous guitar players, like Dweezil Zappa, Eddie Van Halen, and Peter Frampton. They were all there . . . and Christopher

Guest came out as Nigel Tufnel and the others were so excited to be around him.

"They all started telling war stories about when they were touring in England, and what happened when Spinal Tap opened for them. And they were just making up these stories, and Christopher Guest went right along with it, saying things like, 'Remember when this happened?' It was really funny.

"He also gave an extensive interview about what he'd been doing between the time of *Spinal Tap* and this moment," Smokler remembers. "And I have that tape somewhere. He said that somehow he was in the Swiss Army and all that he had left was this piece of military equipment . . . which was a Swiss Army knife. And he would pull each object out of the knife and riff on it for five minutes . . . the corkscrew, the scissors. . . ."

This Is Spinal Tap may not exactly be an embrace, but it's not without sympathy for the genre it parodies, and that may make all the difference in terms of its popularity.

3. It's a paragon of the cult film.

A third theory involves *This Is Spinal Tap* as a quintessential cult film. *Newsday* published an article in November 2005 establishing and enumerating the "unifying traits" of these movies. A cult movie, the article suggested, "should be off-kilter and slightly surreal; it should be tongue-in-cheek, at least a little dirty, and aimed at a (14-year-old giggling boy level); it should have catchphrases everyone likes to quote," and finally it should feature "hapless characters getting into trouble or otherwise operating outside the range of normal."[7]

That's a useful definition, and one can see how *This Is Spinal Tap* (along with the other choices, including *Waiting for Guffman* and *The Rocky Horror Picture Show* [1975]) fit the bill. *Tap* is certainly off kilter, its unmistakable cinema verité form echoing the rock 'n' roll content.

Is it surreal? In a way, yes, because the band Spinal Tap certainly seems bedeviled by bad luck. Inescapable bad luck.

The film also evidences a tongue-in-cheek nature, of course, with the improvisers understanding precisely how far to carry each joke. And it's certainly a bit naughty, especially if you factor in the inflammatory cold sores.

But where *This Is Spinal Tap* truly excels as a cult movie is that it has probably spawned more catchphrases than any other film in motion picture history. The amp going up to eleven (recently voted one of the greatest lines in film history by the American Film Institute), the fine line between stupid and clever, the dusting for vomit, Derek's lukewarm water bit, David's admission that he believes virtually everything he reads, which he suggests makes him a more discerning person than others, and on and on.

Going back to the listed criteria, you simply can't get much more hapless than getting lost backstage, finding yourself trapped in a translucent egg, or playing second fiddle to dwarves, midgets, and puppets.

Voila—instant cult film! "The film's miniature Stonehenge fiasco," noted *The Canberra Times* in Australia, "is as widely quoted by comedy fans as the Monty Python dead parrot skit."[8]

4. All around the world, the same song: or, it's the music.

A fourth reason for *Spinal Tap*'s survival in an ever-changing, ever-faster world of pop culture involves the music industry itself. Musicians, whether they are working in pop, rock, country, or hip-hop, just never change.

Witness Britney Spears mindlessly, vacuously popping bubble gum in Michael Moore's *Fahrenheit 911* (2004), saying that she believes everyone should trust President Bush completely. Witness Jessica Simpson on *Newlyweds: Nick and Jessica* (2003–05) pondering whether Chicken of the Sea is tuna or chicken. Witness the members of Metallica enduring an explosive intervention and intense group therapy in 2004's *Metallica: Some Kind of Monster*.

This Is Spinal Tap remains timely because none of this has changed. At all. And therefore, the film hasn't really aged in the sense one might expect.

"It still holds up today," Chadwick affirms. "I think rock 'n' rollers are still the same. It's based on stories that actually happened and still actually happen. The wardrobe doesn't date it. There's nothing that dates it, except for the fact that it dates itself when it goes back to the sixties and stuff like that."

5. It's unrelentingly smart.

Another reason for the film's continued success is that *Spinal Tap* seems to function on many levels simultaneously. On a simple level, one can just laugh at the funny jokes, which really require no deep knowledge of the rock industry. On the second level, if you know rock music, the movie is even more hilarious. Finally, if you know the tenets of documentary filmmaking, you can watch *Spinal Tap* and see how expertly the film plays with the form.

Many scholars have written lengthy dissertations on *This Is Spinal Tap* and its deeper significance. A decade ago, Carl Plantinga's "Gender, Power and a Cucumber: Satirizing Masculinity in *This Is Spinal Tap*" provided an in-depth analysis of the methods by which the film "uses satire to examine and critique heavy metal generally, and in particular, its promotion of a 'hypermasculine' mythology, an ethos which reduces sexuality to animal instincts, devalues feminine qualities, and excludes women."[9]

6. It is original.

Yet another important factor in *Spinal Tap*'s popularity is its utter originality. "*This Is Spinal Tap* is a very special, very original hoot," wrote David Ansen for *Newsweek*. "Given a target as wide and vulgar as heavy-metal rock, the surprise is that the movie's wit manages to be so subtle."[10]

Although mockumentaries had appeared long before *This Is Spinal Tap*, including Orson Welles' 1938 radio broadcast of *War of the Worlds*, *This Is Spinal Tap* was really the first to so thoroughly mirror both the form and content of a popular movie form (the rock documentary) and satirize it with such dexterity.

"Certainly, we saw a wave of people trying to do—let's not be kind—a rip-off of *Spinal Tap*,"[11] Harry Shearer reported to Craig D. Lindsey of *The News and Observer* during the Full Frame Documentary Film Festival in 2004. Shearer also noted that since *This Is Spinal Tap* premiered in 1984, there had been a country *Spinal Tap*, a hip-hop *Spinal Tap*, and more.

7. They did it best.

Perhaps *This Is Spinal Tap* remains popular because whenever everybody joins the trend and tries to do one of these things, press attention inevitably returns to that gold standard, the high-water mark of the form. You can't make a mockumentary (especially about a rock group) today without a critic bringing up *Spinal Tap*. In fact, the movie is more ubiquitous than even that last sentence suggests: it's also accurate that you can't make a rock documentary today without a critic bringing up *This Is Spinal Tap*.

8. We love the eighties.

I've always believed too that *This Is Spinal Tap* succeeds because it both recalls and embodies the peculiar Zeitgeist of the mid-eighties, the zenith of the glitzy and callow Reagan age. Specifically, the film picks up on the inherent gulf between reality and fiction so dominant in The Gipper's America. It reflects that gulf to a particularly high degree.

Consider the fortieth President of the United States and his nature, just for a moment. Reagan swept into office with the twin goals of shrinking the federal bureaucracy and cutting taxes. But his administration actually added 61,000 federal employees to the government's roster over two terms, and he raised taxes in 1983, 1984, and 1986. In fact, the Tax Reform Act of 1986, signed into law by Reagan, was the biggest tax hike in American history up to that point.

Likewise, the conservative Reagan espoused traditional values, yet he was the nation's first and only divorced president.

President Reagan was always hailed as "The Great Communicator," but his remarks tended to consist of embarrassing non sequiturs. For instance, the commander-in-chief once stated his belief that trees caused environmental pollution. On another occasion, he declared that ketchup was a vegetable.

Reagan also claimed that homeless people were homeless "by choice" and even opined (in his televised debate with Democratic presidential candidate Walter Mondale) that nuclear missiles could be recalled after launch. Of course, that was not the case.

Then there was the time he referred to Princess Diana as Princess David. Or the time he claimed memories of liberating the concentration camps in World War II, when in fact he had never left the United States during that conflict.

In other words, part of "Reagan's success as a leader lay in the fact that much of the myths he created were preferable to reality."[12] This sort of mythmaking was evident in other cultural phenomena of the MTV decade as well. For instance, an early film hit was *Flashdance* (1983), a movie in which an athletic stunt double performed many of the Jennifer Beal character's fanciest moves. It wasn't always easy to detect in the movie's quick-cut editing style, but there it was. In other words, audiences were seeing a movie about a dancer who could not, in any real sense, perform as required of her. Instead, it was all—like Reagan's imagery—a carefully, beautifully crafted, but egregious lie.

Now consider *Spinal Tap* again. The musicians in the group consider themselves to be great classical artists (and even reference Mozart to connect themselves to such greatness), but clearly they are opportunistic hacks who have attempted to exploit every rock trend and tradition since the 1960s, from the Beatles in the 1960s to flower power in the 1970s to heavy metal in the 1980s.

The members of Spinal Tap claim to embody a sense of assertive "power" (with both their chords and mock poses of strength) but are revealed, to a dramatic extent, to be almost totally impotent. Nigel falls down onstage and can't get up until supported by a helpful roadie. Derek becomes trapped in an embryonic pod onstage.

Another symbol of "rock hard" strength, the Stonehenge monument, is reduced, in the band's presence, to a minuscule size . . . its power wholly negated. To be upstaged by dwarves is not merely embarrassing, it is emasculating.

Another illusion, put simply, is the size of Derek's crotch package. As Gloria Gifford's security screener discovers, Derek is not packing heat down there, just an aluminum foil-wrapped vegetable. The imposing, powerful image and illusion of sexual vitality is once more compromised by less-impressive reality.

Reality is constantly reshaped throughout the film, mostly so that the members of Spinal Tap can save face. Manager Ian Faith claims falsely that Boston isn't a "big college town" when the gig is canceled there, an obvious distortion. At another point, when faced with facts that imply the band is losing fans and support, Faith responds with a euphemism, suggesting the band's appeal is simply becoming "more selective." The narrator is unlikely to argue, given that Faith is manhandling a club at this point.

Even *This Is Spinal Tap*'s very format—that of a mockumentary—seems to suggest the idea of egregious mythmaking at the expense of reality. The movie walks and talks like an authentic documentary about a real band—right down to the assumption of all qualities of "direct cinema"—but everything about that band is faked. All the people are actors and the movie is a comedy, not an authentic excavation of truth. A format created explicitly for truth-telling has been humorously subverted for the opposite purpose.

As viewers, are asked to countenance and accept this gap. We are asked to process the gulf between reality and illusion, and—even more amazingly—to find the truth of the band's journey underneath the central deception. And here's the rub: in lying, we must wonder, does *This Is Spinal Tap* tell the truth more fully than standard documentaries about the rock world? Is that a paradox? To paraphrase Tap, do two lies make a truth?

Okay, now I'm just confusing myself, but I think you get the point. In incident and form, *This Is Spinal Tap* appears to mimic the central quality of the Reagan era.

And if we return to Harry Shearer's epitaph for 1980s rock quality, "the music has left the building," it's yet another layer of artifice separating truth from the illusion—specifically, the dead (or dying) belief of the corporate Reagan era—during which yuppies traded antigovernment protest and antiwar sentiment for stock options and a corner office—that rock music could change the world.

Yet in fact, Spinal Tap's music has no socially redeeming value. Instead, the band wallows in juvenilia and in so-called "retarded sexuality." As Brian Fitzpatrick noted in a review of Spinal Tap's *Back from the Dead*, the band "uses all the clichés of rock music" and "creative yet stereotypical lyrics often about mystical, demon or sexual topics sung with the backing of a screeching/yelling lead singer, a temperamental lead guitarist and a silent, almost Zen bass player."[13]

In this fashion, *This Is Spinal Tap* seems an ideal time capsule of the 1980s. It acknowledges that people—when faced with cold, hard facts—will select a pleasant illusion every time. Sometimes the lies we tell ourselves are preferable to hard truths. And this may be an acceptable way to live (or make a terrific movie), yet it's certainly a lousy way to run a country. In the gap between truth and self-delusion, perhaps, we see something of ourselves, and our common humanity.

9. The final chapter is yet unwritten.

This Is Spinal Tap also remains a popular cult movie, I submit, because many of us sense the story isn't quite over yet. On television, we've seen aging rockers like Gene Simmons and Ozzy Osbourne move on to their third acts and deal with the reality of being senior citizens. There was even a movie on that subject, Brian Gibson's 1998 effort *Still Crazy*. It featured a band called Strange Fruit getting back together after breaking up in the 1990s. The performers were in their fifties.

As the rockers of the 1970s move into the geriatric realm yet stay in the public eye, one wonders what the next incarnation of *Spinal Tap* will look like. A reality show set in The Ruins, the Tufnel castle? Or one that features the St. Hubbins children?

The joke goes on, and *Spinal Tap* lives. As Gary Arnold so tellingly wrote in *The Washington Post* when *Spinal Tap* premiered, "There'll always be a gig out there, somewhere. . . ."[14]

10. *This Is Spinal Tap* is a self-help guide to life.

This unique theory comes from a reader of *The New York Times*, who sent a letter to the paper on September 17, 2000 (which was printed on page 4), stating that *This Is Spinal Tap* possesses many of the answers to coping with life's difficulties.

For instance, the writer suggests that remarks such as "I'll rise above it, I'm a professional," and "It's a problem; it gets solved" possess a deep, if simple, sense of wisdom.

Indeed, blending cleverness and stupidity, don't they?

11. The powers that be should be made to smell their glove.

Finally, in some self-reflexive, meta-postmodern fashion, *This Is Spinal Tap* represents the triumph of the little guy in a difficult situation. I don't just mean the band—I mean the people who brought the movie to us in the first place.

"We're really proud of *Spinal Tap*," Shearer reports, "because we basically had to will that film into being. There was absolutely no encouragement and no understanding, with the exception of Norman Lear, who said, 'Okay,' fled the scene, and left the company [Embassy]. So we were just pushing the rug uphill all the time, and I think we're entitled to feel a little vindicated that we were right and all those assholes were wrong."[15]

Looking across the TV and movie landscape today, where mockumentaries seem to reign, one might conclude that time has finally caught up with *This Is Spinal Tap* and the form it pioneered in 1984 has been accepted by the masses. That's undoubtedly true, but *This Is Spinal Tap* remains the cherished progenitor.

In fact, *This Is Spinal Tap* continues to be referenced on an almost daily basis (on *Veronica Mars* [2005], on *House* [2005], in *Spider-Man 3* [2007], and even by the "demi-gods of Canadian metal" in *Anvil! The Story of Anvil* [2007]).

As Carly Simon might note at this juncture, "nobody does it better." And that's a fact as true of *This Is Spinal Tap* now as it was in 1984.

CHAPTER 5

Spinal Tap Moments
For Real . . .

One of the (many) pop culture touchstones that emerged from *This Is Spinal Tap* is the terrifying notion of a "*Spinal Tap* moment*,*" widely defined as a public humiliation wherein something like stagecraft or a personal appearance goes horribly, terribly, utterly wrong.

Anyone who has been before the public eye even briefly has likely experienced the proverbial *Spinal Tap* moment. Politicians, authors, rock stars, news anchors—it doesn't matter. It happens to the best of us.

For instance, I distinctly recall a fancy book signing some years back when nobody at the bookstore (in a rural Southern town)—and I mean nobody—showed the slightest interest in purchasing my book. My wife and I did get free coffees during the two and a half hours of misery and public shame, but that seemed precious little consolation.

At the time, my horrified brain cells registered instantly that this was a *Spinal Tap* moment. Specifically, I recalled the band's failed record promotion in the Midwest, courtesy of Artie Fufkin . . . and the stacks of black albums dotting the walls behind them as the group waited in vain for an audience . . . *any audience* . . . to validate their existence.

Whew! That's dark.

Of course, rock 'n' roll, the context from which *This Is Spinal Tap* sprang, has witnessed more than its fair share of such trademark, humiliating instances. Much of this accuracy concerning rock history came from the film's clever creators, who studied it, watched rockumentaries, and attended live performances.

Yet *Tap*'s creators are always quick to state that they did not intend in the film to mock any particular performer or hark back to any specific—and painful—real-life incident. "It has always been a pastiche," Shearer has established on more than one occasion. "There are a lot of people walking around saying, 'That's about us.' That's nice, but it's not true."[1] Rather, the makers of *Tap* are mocking *the whole genre*. That said, Jeff Beck has come out on record and denied that he was Guest's inspiration for Nigel Tufnel. On the contrary, says Beck, only his hairstyle was adopted by *Tap*'s thoughtful guitarist.

Now, for your consideration below is an enumeration of several notorious *Spinal Tap* moments in music history— some of which occurred before the film, some after. But despite the glaring similarities, please keep in mind that any resemblance to any real rocker or group is not intentional and, in fact, entirely coincidental. . . .

Stagecraft

Wherein something goes horribly wrong during a live stage performance.

In *Spinal Tap*, one can pick any variety of embarrassing moments involving stage mechanics, many already mentioned in this text. Derek becomes trapped in a translucent (and veiny) womb/pod during the band's live performance of "Rock and Roll Creation." And while jamming to "Hellhole," Nigel falls down and can't get up until aided by a stalwart roadie, Moke.

Perhaps the strangest and (and funniest) stage problem in *This Is Spinal Tap* involves a stage prop that just isn't designed correctly: the underwhelming Trilithon Horseshoe from Stonehenge. Intended to be eighteen feet high, the final prop stands a meager eighteen inches instead. This necessitates the incorporation of midgets into the production number.

These various and sundry mishaps may sound like wild flights of fancy, but that is not the case. To wit, in 1956, at the

Apollo Theater, Screamin' Jay Hawkin performed "I Put a Spell on You." But he became trapped in a coffin, not unlike Derek's pod, onstage and, in a panic, reportedly lost control of his bowels. Similarly, members of U2 were reportedly stuck inside a giant, forty-foot metallic "pod" during a performance on their 1997 PopMart Tour.

Similarly, Fleetwood Mac in 1997 once had to contend with a seventy-foot penguin balloon float that just wouldn't inflate. Not quite the same thing as Stonehenge . . . but close enough for jazz. Or rock.

Regarding dwarves, rocker Ozzy Osbourne reportedly experienced his own run-in with a midget hired for a Black Sabbath tour. According to George Rush and Joanna Molloy's piece in *The New York Daily News* in May 2005, Osbourne tossed the troublesome dwarf into the luggage compartment of his tour bus.

Another famous mishap in music history includes Bob Dylan's malfunctioning mike in D. A. Pennebaker's landmark film, *Dont Look Back.* But that film may be more famous for the memorable scene in which Dylan becomes lost in the twisting corridors behind the stage of a venue. I wonder, where have we seen that before? The band-lost-behind-the-scenes event also reportedly happened to KOOPA and Def Leppard.

In the most supreme of ironies, apparently Spinal Tap itself experienced a *Spinal Tap* moment involving the stage . . . and getting to it. In 1984, as the movie played in theaters, the band played at CBGB, a punk club on the Lower East Side of New York City. But, according to Steven Rea, who recorded the story in *The Philadelphia Inquirer*, when the band got there, there were no roadies present to set up the equipment.

"So we're standing there—*these 36-year-old guys*—with no manager, no one to lay down the cables, and it was a question of what now? Are we going to unpack these Marshall [amps] and put them on stage or what?"[2] Guest told Rea.

Like I said, it happens to the best of us. . . .

Circular Logic and Pompous Phraseology

Wherein a rocker/musician attempts to say something meaningful and deep, but only succeeds in confusing the audience, and usually himself as well.

The *Spinal Tap* moment proves that profundity is always in the eye of the beholder. Or something.

In *Spinal Tap*, for instance, the band members make their immortal remark about the fine line separating stupid and clever.

Another example of circular logic is Nigel's conversation with Di Bergi about his amp and his inability to understand the director's point, insisting finally that his amps are "one louder" than those that go only to ten.

Again, in the Bob Dylan documentary, *Dont Look Back,* Dylan utters a variety of bizarre and nonsensical statements for the record. He notes that he will "become insane if he becomes insane." (?) He opines that "There are no ideas in *Time* magazine. There's just facts. . . . Every word has its little letter and its big letter." And after one disturbing incident involving a thrown glass, the artist declares, "I don't care who did it. I just want to know who did it."

Similarly, in *The Last Waltz,* Rick Danko of The Band comments on an upcoming performance serving as "a celebration of the beginning of the end of the beginning," displaying the propensity in rock toward circular logic.

Going one step further, Lars Ulrich, the drummer for Metallica, asks in Joe Berlinger's *Some Kind of Monster*: "Where does the record start? Where does it end?" Later he also opines that the band has created "aggressive music without negative energy."

Right.

Well Versed in the Classics

For some reason, there's a focus in many rock docs on a validation of the form of rock 'n' roll itself, as well as its practitioners. It's as though being just a rock star simply isn't good enough. No, one must actually be a *classically trained* musician too.

Such training apparently grants the band or act a shot at greatness for the ages. In other words, this is a plea to the musical establishment and musical elitists to please consider rock 'n' roll a legitimate artistic expression.

In *Spinal Tap,* Marti Di Bergi records a session of Nigel playing a lovely, haunting portion of a newly composed "musical trilogy" at the piano (called "Love Pump"), establishing his credentials as a "serious" artist. Nigel also utilizes a violin in one performance, and discusses his appreciation of Bach and Mozart, synthesizing this love into the unholy thing he calls "Mach." The violin reference apparently involves Led Zeppelin and Jimmy Page, who was wont to play his guitar with a bow.

These moments also feel like an echo of *The Last Waltz*, in which—during "Old Time Religion"—a violin also inevitably gets trotted out. Also, Gaelic is spoken during a concert in the film. The makers of the film might as well yell, "See, rockers are really, really smart!"

Personnel Changes
In which someone in the band dies, leaves, or is replaced.

For Spinal Tap, personnel changes are a frequent problem, since drummers keep dying (by some accounts, approximately thirty drummers for Spinal Tap must have died over the years). Of course, this could be a reference to Keith Moon of the Who. Or John Bonham of Led Zeppelin.

And in *Metallica: Some Kind of Monster*, bassist Jason Newsted quits Metallica after fourteen years (to toil with the younglings at Echobrain) and James Hetfield disappears from studio recording sessions—for fourteen months!—to undergo drug and alcohol rehab.

Recently, it has become virtually impossible to keep track of personnel changes in Aerosmith, with Steve Tyler retiring from the band, then returning.

Jealousy

Wherein members of one band, fearing professional apocalypse, badmouth another act.

In *Spinal Tap*, David, Derek, and Nigel note in a hotel lobby that they've had to apologize for Duke Fame and the Flame Throwers with their fan set on occasion. This exchange occurs after meeting him and learning that he is playing in a large arena, whereas their appearance has been canceled.

In *Dont Look Back,* Bob Dylan notes of an up-and-comer named Donovan: "I already hate him."

'Nuff said.

Diva Madness

Although June Chadwick steadfastly denies that Yoko Ono (or Anita Pallenberg, for that matter) was on in her mind while playing venomous Jeanine Pettibone, there are audience members who persist in seeing her in that very mold. Jeanine is the "opinionated" girlfriend coming into an "all boy's show" to spoil the fun and divide the band.

And that has happened more than once in rock history, hasn't it?

CHAPTER 6

The "Where Are They Now" File
The Makers of *This Is Spinal Tap*
Twenty-five Years Later

In *This Is Spinal Tap*, a radio DJ plays a track from Spinal Tap's 1960s Beatles-like incarnation entitled "Cups and Cakes," much to the delight of a nostalgic Nigel and David. But delight turns to horror when the radio man adds that Spinal Tap currently resides in the "Where Are They Now File."

Below, in a totally nonpejorative sense, are twenty "Where Are They Now File" updates on the talents behind this cult movie and where they stand now.

Christopher Guest: After a string of mockumentary (er, *documentary-style*) comedies in the 1990s and early 2000s (*Waiting for Guffman*, *Best in Show*, and *A Mighty Wind*), Guest returned as director, cowriter (with Eugene Levy), and actor in his latest film project, the poorly received *For Your Consideration* (2006).

Working with his cast of regulars, including McKean, Shearer, Fred Willard, and Parker Posey, as well as newcomers such as Ricky Gervais (of BBC's edgy *The Office*), Guest's latest project involved a group of actors in a very bad film (*Home for Purim*) who mistakenly assume they'll be nominated for prominent industry awards.

Following appearances in *Night at the Museum: Battle of the Smithsonian* (2009) and *The Invention of Lying* (2009), Guest directed a commercial in the mockumentary mode for the U.S. Census starring Bob Balaban and Ed Begley Jr. It aired during the February 2010 Super Bowl and was the subject of some controversy because many deemed it unfunny.

Michael McKean: After appearing as one of the Folksmen (with Shearer and Guest) in *A Mighty Wind,* this busy talent appeared on Broadway in 2004, playing Edna Turnblad in *Hairspray*, replacing Harvey Fierstein.

McKean has also appeared as Perry White in the WB series *Smallville*, which costarred his wife, Annette O'Toole, for several seasons. He's also been a guest star on series including David E. Kelley's *Boston Legal* (2005), where he played a husband who had carnal knowledge of a goat. On cult hits *The*

Lone Gunmen (2001) and *The X-Files* (1993–2002), McKean played Morris Fletcher, a covert operative who claimed responsibility for inventing Saddam Hussein.

Rob Reiner: The director of *This Is Spinal Tap* has had an impressive career that includes cult hits such as *The Princess Bride* (1987) and blockbuster hits like *A Few Good Men* (1992). Reiner recently directed *Rumor Has It . . .* (2005) and *The Bucket List* (2007).

A leading progressive voice in California politics, Rob Reiner is often mentioned as a future candidate for governor of that state. In 2010, he received an American Cinema Editors Golden Eddie Filmmaker of the Year award. It was presented to him by his longtime friend, Christopher Guest.

Harry Shearer: After directing his own comedy feature, *Teddy Bears' Picnic* (2002), this talented actor, comedian, and commentator returned to voice-over work on the long-running Fox hit *The Simpsons*, and also provided a voice for the animated hit *Chicken Little* (2005) and *The Simpsons Movie* (2007).

Following Hurricane Katrina and the disaster in New Orleans, Shearer's blog about reconstruction, reform, and corruption in the storm's aftermath has become required reading on *The Huffington Post*.

In 2008 and 2009 Shearer was nominated for a Grammy Award in the category Best Comedy Album (for *Songs Pointed & Pointless* and *Songs of the Bushmen*). In 2009, he was also nominated for a Primetime Emmy Award for his outstanding voice contributions to *The Simpsons*.

Ed Begley Jr.: This actor appeared in *A Mighty Wind* as PBN network executive Lars Olfen, and more recently completed work on a trio of films including *The Optimist* (2005), *Tripping Forward* (2006), and *Making Change* (2006).

Paul Benedict: This onetime star of TV's *The Jeffersons* (1975–85) appeared in *A Mighty Wind* in 2003 and *After the Sunset* in 2004. He passed away December 1, 2008.

Kent Beyda: The film editor on such eighties favorites as *Spinal Tap* and *Fright Night* (1985) recently edited *Scooby Doo 2: Monsters Unleashed* (2005), *Garfield 2* (2006), and *Jonah Hex* (2010).

June Chadwick: David St. Hubbin's ladylove, Jeanine, provided voice-over work for the *Star Trek* video game *Away Team* (2002), and in 2004, sci-fi fans could relish her slithery performance as the alien Visitor commander, Lydia, in the DVD Box Set release of the 1980s cult original *V: The Series*.

Billy Crystal: The frequent Academy Awards host recently contributed his voice to films such as *Monsters, Inc.* (2001) and *Cars* (2006).

Fran Drescher: After years of success on the popular sitcom *The Nanny* (1993–99), Fran Drescher created the TV pilot *Living with Fran.* In 1989, she also appeared in Christopher Guest's directing debut, *The Big Picture.* In 2008, Drescher became Public Diplomacy Envoy for Women's Health Issues at the behest of the U.S. State Department.

Gloria Gifford: This remarkable veteran of eighties cult movies such as *D.C. Cab* (1983) completed a film with Margaret Cho, directed a production at Carnegie Hall in 2005, writes at the American Film Institute, and runs The Gloria Gifford Conservatory for Performing Arts, a Professional Acting, Directing, Writing Arena.

Tony Hendra: The actor who portrayed Ian Faith, the hapless manager of Spinal Tap, in 2004 published a best-selling memoir entitled *Father Joe.* In 2005, his daughter published a rebuttal of sorts entitled *How to Cook Your Daughter: A Memoir.* Lawsuits for everybody. . . .

Howard Hesseman: This actor recently appeared in *About Schmidt* (2002) with Jack Nicholson; Harry Shearer's comedy, *Teddy Bears' Picnic* (2002); and Rob Zombie's horror sequel, *Halloween 2* (2009).

Anjelica Huston: The daughter of late director John Huston continues a stellar career in feature films, with recent appearances in films such as *The Life Aquatic with Steve Zissou* (2004) with Bill Murray. In 2008–09, she had a recurring role on the psychic mystery series *Medium*.

Bruno Kirby: Once Spinal Tap's "Jimmy," this beloved *City Slickers* (1991) actor played Los Angeles prosecutor Vincent Bugliosi in the 2004 TV movie about Charles Manson, *Helter Skelter*. Kirby passed away on August 14, 2006.

Robert Leighton: *This Is Spinal Tap*'s supervising editor continues to be Rob Reiner's go-to guy for editing, having cut his films *The Bucket List* (2007), *Rumor Has It . . .* (2005), and *Alex & Emma* (2003).

Patrick Macnee: *Spinal Tap*'s ebullient Sir Denis recently starred in *The Low Budget Time Machine* (2003) and had a cameo in the big-screen version of his popular 1960s TV series, *The Avengers* (1998).

Karen Murphy: *Spinal Tap*'s producer also produced *Waiting for Guffman, Best in Show, A Mighty Wind*, and Guest's latest project, *For Your Consideration.*

Kim Secrist: An editor on *Spinal Tap*, Secrist is a sound editor on such high-profile Hollywood projects as *Stealth* (2005) and *Collateral* (2004).

Paul Shaffer: Shaffer, who so memorably asked to have his "ass kicked" in *Spinal Tap*, remains the longtime music supervisor and onscreen sidekick of late-night talk show host David Letterman on CBS's *The Late Show.*

Peter Smokler: *Spinal Tap*'s cinematographer has been busy shooting TV series, including the pilots for *It's Always Sunny in Philadelphia* (2005) and NBC's *The Office* (2005). Smokler has also served as the director of photography on the hit series *Parks and Recreation* (2009), the Freddie Prinze sitcom *Freddie* (2005), and *George Lopez* (2007).

Fred Willard: After his hilarious turn as announcer Buck Laughlin in *Best in Show* (2000), Willard repeated his success in *A Mighty Wind* and Guest's latest opus, *For Your Consideration*. Willard has provided voice-over work for animated films including *Chicken Little* (2005) and *Cat Tale* (2006), and appeared in the hit Will Ferrell comedy, *Anchorman: The Legend of Ron Burgundy* (2004) as well as the critically acclaimed Pixar animated film, *Wall-E* (2008).

NOTES

1

1. Patrick Douglas, "Mysteries of *This Is Spinal Tap* Finally Decoded," *Fort Collins Coloradoan,* May 13, 2005, 12E.

2. *Entertainment Weekly,* "The 100 Funniest Movies on Video: Mirth of a Nation," October 16, 1992, 16.

3. Pamela McClintock, "'Boyz,' 'Alien,' 'Spinal' Tapped for Film Registry (U.S. Library of Congress' National Film Registry)," *Daily Variety,* December 18, 2002, 4–5.

4. McClintock, "'Boyz,' 'Alien,' 'Spinal' Tapped for Film Registry," 4–5.

5. Richard Corliss, "Cinema: Cold Metal," *Time,* March 5, 1984, 86.

6. John Leland, "The Heavy Metal Joke Not Everyone Got," *The New York Times.* September 3, 2000, 22.

7. Archer Winsten, *The New York Post,* March 2, 1984, 19.

8. Michael Blowen, "Rob Reiner Has the Last Laugh," *The Boston Globe*, May 3, 1984, Calendar, 1.

9. Fred Phillips, "After 20 Years, '*Spinal Tap*' Still Rocks," *The Monroe News-Star*, July 8, 2004, 9d.

10. Michael Blowen, "Exclusive!!! *Spinal Tap* Debunks Rockumentary!" *The Boston Globe*, July 5, 1984, Calendar, 2 of 4.

2

1. James Parker, "Rockumentary 101: *This Is Spinal Tap* Gave Us the Term Rockumentary in 1984, and Then Almost Killed the Genre with Its Lethal Satire. Now a New Film Proves What a Rockumentary Can Do—and It's Less *Spinal Tap* Than *Let It Be*," *The Boston Globe*, August 22, 2004, F2.

2. Matthew Gilbert, "Mockumentaries Show Reality for What It Is," *The Boston Globe*, February 14, 2001, Home, Arts and Entertainment Section, http://www.boston.com/ae/tv/articles/2010/02/14/mockumentary_as_sitcome_is_an_art_complementary_to_televisions_format/.

3

1. Louis B. Hobson, "Guest Shots," *Edmonston Sun*, October 10, 2000.

2. John Kenneth Muir, *Best in Show: The Films of Christopher Guest and Company* (New York: Applause Theatre and Film Books, 2004).

3. Richard Meran Bersam, *Non-Fiction Film: A Critical History* (Bloomington, IN: Clarke, Irwin and Company, Ltd., 1973), 303.

4. Bersam, *Non-Fiction Film*, 2–4.

5. John Kenneth Muir, *The Rock and Roll Film Encyclopedia* (New York: Applause Theatre and Cinema Books, 2007), 115.

6. Josh Goldfein, "Band of Outsidersm" *The Village Voice*. April 10–16, 2002.

7. Karl French, *This Is Spinal Tap: The Official Companion* (London and New York: Bloomsbury, 2000), 206.

8. Christopher Guest, Michael McKean, Rob Reiner, and Harry Shearer, *Spinal Tap* (Los Angeles: Spinal Tap Productions, 1982), 5.

9. Guest, McKean, Reiner, Shearer, *Spinal Tap,* 25.

10. Guest, McKean, Reiner, Shearer, *Spinal Tap,* 37.

11. Frank N. Magill, ed., *Magill's Cinema Annual, 1985: A Survey of 1984 Films* (New York: Salem Press, 1985), 487.

4

1. Bill Cosford,"Spinal Tap Slices up Rock," *The Miami Herald,* April 27, 1984, 1D.

2. Steve Morse, "Spinal Tap Socks It to Rock," *The Boston Globe*, March 30, 1984, Section Arts/Films.

3. Gene Triplett, "Mockumentary May Tap Too Closely to Heart of Rock 'n' Roll to Be Funny," *The Daily Oklahoman.* May 25, 1984, Section NEWS.

4. "Creating Spinal Tap," *The New York Times,* June 20, 2004, Section 7, Column 4, Book Review Desk, 4.

5. Joe Baltake, "Putting on the Rockers," *Philadelphia Daily News,* May 7, 1984, 35.

6. Wayne Robins, *Newsday.* March 2, 1984, II,:6.

7. "The Kings of Cult Classics," *Chicago Tribune*, November 1, 2005, 29.

8. "Parody Gained Cult Status," *The Canberra Times,* August 7, 2005, A22.

9. Barry Keith Grant and Jeanette Sloniowski, eds., *Documenting the Documentary: Close Readings of Documentary Film and Video* (Detroit: Wayne State University Press, 1998), 319–327.

10. David Ansen, *Newsweek,* March 5, 1984, 81.

11. Craig D. Lindsey, "Shearer Goes for Real Laughs," *The News and Observer*, April 2, 2004, WUP5.

12. Jane Mayer and Doyle McManus, *Landslide: The Unmaking of the President, 1984-1988* (Boston: Houghton Mifflin, 1988), 11.

13. Brian Fitzpatrick, "Music Review: *Spinal Tap—Back from the Dead* (CD/DVD)," *Blogcritics,* June 23, 2009, http://blogcritics.org/music/article/music-review-spinal-tap-back-from/.

14. Gary Arnold, "Spinal Chords," *The Washington Post*, April 13, 1984, B1.

15. John Kenneth Muir, *The Rock and Roll Film Encyclopedia* (New York: Applause Theatre and Cinema Books, 2007), 275.

5

1. Tasha Robinson, "Interview with Harry Shearer," *The Onion AV Club* 9 (15) (April 23, 2003).

2. Stephen Rea, "Christopher Guest: From *Spinal Tap* to *Best in Show*," *Knight Ridder/Tribune News Service*, October 6, 2000, K438.

INDEX